THE MICHAEL SCHOOL

The Archangel Michael
(twelfth century)

THE
MICHAEL SCHOOL

And the School of
Spiritual Science

Peter Selg

STEINERBOOKS | 2016

STEINERBOOKS
An imprint of Anthroposophic Press, Inc.
610 Main St., Great Barrington, MA 01230
www.steinerbooks.org

Translated by Matthew Barton

Book design by William Jens Jensen

LIBRARY OF CONGRESS CONTROL NUMBER: 2016944810

ISBN: 978-1-62148-155-3 (paperback)
ISBN: 978-1-62148-156-0 (ebook)

Contents

Foreword

We must regard this School as constituted directly out of the will of the world of spirit itself, modified only insofar as an effort is made to interpret it in the right way for the era we entered when the age of darkness was over and a light returned—though as yet this still comes to imperfect expression on Earth since people perpetuate the old darkness. But the light is here. And only if we understand that it is now present again will we fully grasp the nature and intent of this, our school of the spirit.

RUDOLF STEINER, March 21, 1924[1]

This monograph returns to themes I explored in my book *Rudolf Steiner and the School of Spiritual Science: The Foundation of the "First Class,"*[2] as well as various other studies connected with the theme of the Christmas Foundation Meeting and refounding the School. These historically significant matters also have important implications for the present and future. My account deals primarily with the relationship between the esoteric school at the Goetheanum and the Michael movement, whose destiny and global mission Rudolf Steiner elaborated upon in detail in his 1924 lectures on karma. It seems to me important to outline connections between the refounding of Society and School, the karma lectures, the Leading Thoughts and the First Class, focusing more narrowly on this context and thus making it more accessible to those, particularly, who seek entry to the School of Spiritual Science or wish to deepen an already existing relationship with it. As becomes evident in conversations and seminars, members often have only a tenuous awareness of these contexts, which in consequence fail to inspire their commitment or strength of connection with them. In many anthroposophic centers, too, there is a tendency to regard the Class lessons or the group of people who hold and listen to them, as an autonomous entity existing (for the time being still) at one remove from other anthroposophic activities and gatherings.

The esoteric school at the Goetheanum and its First Class, however, have an intimate and intrinsic connection with the spiritual, social, and cultural impulse at the heart of the Christmas Foundation Meeting, and should retain this connection. As well as being one of Rudolf Steiner's prime concerns for further anthroposophic work, this also arises naturally from the specific content and aims of such work. If common awareness of what was initiated and founded in 1923/24 grows among members of the General Anthroposophical Society in future, its activities can successfully be furthered despite all the obstacles and difficulties we encounter. This includes work on the core mantric content of the Class lessons, which we should recognize as being of extraordinary relevance, *not only* for specific professions and areas of expertise but also in a general human sense, and in relation to all human society.

We know that Rudolf Steiner described the esoteric school at the Goetheanum as the center of the General Anthroposophical Society and the Dornach School with all its professional departments (sections). He repeatedly emphasized the spiritual strength that would be required in future for a person to maintain his individuality and be able to carry Anthroposophy into diverse domains of civilization. But this spiritual strength—which is urgently needed today in the General Anthroposophical Society and the diverse fields of work—is primarily to be found by living with the mantras of the First Class.

In what follows, the *form* of the esoteric Class lessons will be mentioned only in passing, particularly in the chapter on Ita Wegman. In 2008, it was my concern to show that holding the Class lessons given by Rudolf Steiner in their original wording should by no means be regarded too hastily as a distortion of his "original intentions"[3] and to be thus eliminated either intentionally or unintentionally, consciously or unconsciously, from the anthroposophic movement. I have shown how difficult it is to determine clearly what Rudolf Steiner's "original" intentions were, or even his core intention.[4]

It is likewise a tendentious simplification to distinguish between "free renderings" of the lessons on the one hand and ("unfree") readings of the lessons, without discussing in detail the questions and challenges connected with both undertakings. In my exploration of the destiny and Class work of Ita Wegman, I tried to show the spiritual significance of holding a Class lesson in the wording by Steiner, in inner connection with him, or of adopting a "free" stance toward the content of the lesson, that is, to produce this content out of one's own "I" and to take responsibility for it through and with this "I." Thereupon a "restorative or conservative intent" was ascribed both to my commentary and to me myself. It was thought my aim was to establish a kind of liturgy read by appointed, priest-type figures, and that I was unwilling to concede that a "lecture scenario" had long since been replaced by "free discussion and enquiry in research groups and communities." This latter was thought to be the *only possible* developmental direction for Anthroposophy to pursue, and the only one in tune with modern consciousness.[5]

This "restorative intent," as has been written most recently, is regarded as the outlook of a conservative group of people whose retrograde, devotional stance testifies to a fear of "holding free Class lessons, let alone engaging in discussions about the contents of the School."[6] No attention was given at all to the content of my presentations on various related themes and issues. And yet it will be a key task of the future to understand the severe limits of an outlook based on polar distinctions between "preserving and handing down a stream of revelation" on the one hand, and an "individualized esotericism" on the other (J. Kiersch). This is to underestimate the real challenge we face, or wilfully oversimplify it.

In my view it is self-evident—and requires no further debate—that passive reading of the Class lesson text, and passive listening to it, in however dignified a form, is quite definitely *not* the aim of the First Class and its path of schooling. Ludwig Polzer-Hoditz, a man of great wisdom and experience, drew attention to this fact as long ago as 1935. ("It is...certainly not in accord with his [Rudolf Steiner's] intention, nor is it Michaelic, simply to read the Class lessons aloud in dogmatic fashion."[7]) Yet for over ninety years now, countless Class members have witnessed (also in lessons led by Polzer-Hoditz himself) all that can come about and come into movement in a lesson given in Rudolf Steiner's wording in so far as this is not merely read out and listened to passively but held instead in a really active way, with people who fully and actively participate. These people have experienced the grandeur and significance of the original lessons and their content, in its connection with the spiritual world of the hierarchies, with Michael, with the reality of the anthroposophic movement, the spiritual presence of Rudolf Steiner *and* with their own being. Both during and after these lessons they have initiated esoteric work on the (mantric and other) content of the texts, and cultivated an "individualized" (or "individualizing") esotericism.

In addition to holding Class lesson readings (seen in *this* light and shaped accordingly), Ita Wegman internationally facilitated and promoted gatherings dedicated to work on the mantras, as well as free lessons, as understood today, in which the people holding them were urged to present the results of their own work on the mantras (in addition to the mantras themselves). It is clear that such a challenge encouraged and encourages individuals to be creatively productive. Holding and shaping a free lesson today remains one of the most helpful ways of engaging with this mantric content. Since the time of Jørgen Smit, and inspired by him, numerous anthroposophists have taken on this challenge and benefited from it. Over and above this, it has increasingly proven possible to relate the specific content and mantras of the Class lessons to diverse professions, and to establish corresponding working groups and communities—most recently for instance also in an anthroposophic clinic.

All this work is extremely positive and of very great importance for the future. It is significant that Johannes Kiersch, in his painstaking archive studies, has been able to determine (among many other discoveries) how early this productive activity of many intermediaries began in different countries.

It is quite another thing however to promote the assumption that holding a Class lesson in the wording by Rudolf Steiner is inevitably a discredited activity, irrespective of the quality invested in such work. I agree entirely with Johannes Kiersch that "Rudolf Steiner, when developing the School, was concerned from the very beginning to make each new esoteric lesson into a new event, and an approach to the living world of spirit"[8]—and I believe this remains the concern of every Class lesson to this day. Nevertheless, *the way Michael brings the past to effect in a present human life*[9] is extremely diverse and varied.

Here it is worth proceeding in a differentiated way rather than waving banners of conservatism versus innovation, or revelation stream versus individualized esotericism. Such entrenched positions are alien to Anthroposophy and harm our common concerns. Lessons read in the wording by Steiner *can* degrade into a passive lecture, becoming rigidly dogmatic and thus anti-Michaelic. They can likewise become the power instrument of a privileged group or institution. On the other hand, instead of being esoteric events that "approach the living world of spirit," the free lessons can become (even if well-meaning) anthroposophic lectures or contributions connected rather more with the speaker than with the intent of the nineteen lessons themselves that Rudolf Steiner held after the Christmas Foundation Meeting. These lessons are a unique treasure, of incomparable and vital worth, not only as regards their mantric content but also in their linguistic composition—as Class members throughout the world know who have *heard* and *experienced* them in a Class group.

Thus the Class lessons are—inevitably—a treasure over which conflict wages. At a gathering, in Dornach in April

1990, of the Anthroposophical Society's General Secretaries and executive councils from different countries, Jørgen Smit described the ahrimanic and luciferic threat to the School[10] in a very striking and in some respects prophetic way, then stated: "The whole activity of the School of Spiritual Science is exposed to this...attack, the pressure of which can only be overcome through spiritual activity from within."[11] He spoke of the need to wake up to the *"full reality of the Michael School's task for humanity,"*[12] one that he himself worked intensively and very successfully to further. Eighteen years later (in 2008) Sergei O. Prokofieff stressed that the core of the work of the Class lessons was about intensifying the presence and influence of Michael—*through* the lessons, in each individual's spiritualized thinking, in the vessel of the community, and in its consequent effect upon civilization:

> ...At the center of every properly held...Class lesson, and solely capable of giving it esoteric significance, is the possibility created by those present of allowing Michael himself to be present in this spiritual work. Here lies the central importance of the Class lessons—one that, alongside other tasks relating to a more personal path of schooling, should definitely not be overlooked or forgotten.[13]

Sergei O. Prokofieff did not by any means see this presence of the Archai Michael, the time spirit, in terms only of a spiritual atmosphere in the room where a lesson is held. In his magnificent studies on the First Class, and in a wide-ranging and profound work on Michael, he pointed during the last phase of his creative work on Earth to the nature of the Michaelic path that human consciousness can pursue both in and with these lessons, and to the form of a Christ–Michael community that can develop in consequence. Prokofieff, who himself held most impressive free lessons but also had an acute perception of the value of lessons held in Rudolf Steiner's wording if these maintained a high level of spiritual activity, here pointed to the future, albeit one that begins in the present.

Until shortly before he died, Rudolf Steiner continued to work on the development of the esoteric school at the Goetheanum and its Classes. He alone could develop and structure this in its consistent, exclusively future-oriented form. All statements that have come down to us from conversations with him should not deceive us about the basic fact that at his death he did not leave any single guideline about how the Class lessons should be held, or how work should be done on their texts. *"Do it as you see fit..."*[14] While still alive, he approved holding (reading) the lessons based on the shorthand transcripts of them—that is, the texts in his wording—for specific groups of people in Prague and Stuttgart; he was also keen that the mantras of the lessons be made known to School members, or in other words communicated to them. In so far as one wishes to or can use this term in this context, his core intention here was for people actually to tread the path of spiritual schooling, rather than for a group of pupils to hold esoteric lessons whether in free or unfree form.

We know that, from the founding of the esoteric school in 1904, Rudolf Steiner held the "esoteric lessons" based on his knowledge and degree as an initiate. The refounding of the school following the Christmas Foundation Meeting did not alter this. Many of his pupils lived with the mantras and exercises of the former esoteric lessons, of which no transcripts were ever made, and whose wording has not survived. For this reason it was not possible for anyone to "repeat" them in later years, either freely or in their original form. It was only because Rudolf Steiner allowed Helene Finckh to make a shorthand transcript of the esoteric lessons after the Christmas Foundation Meeting—so that the exact wording of the texts of all nineteen lessons was preserved—that a new situation arose. After Steiner's death, members of the School had and still have a responsibility to handle these texts with great care. For good reason these members have taken different paths with this, and will continue to do so in future.

The present book aims to reflect and preserve such diversity. As Rudolf Steiner stated: "Try to find peaceful accord with all. It is important now that the Michael stream should make progress. As long as you hold the Class lessons in a serious way, and enrich its content, your work will prosper."[15]

I

The School of Spiritual Science

Michael can give us new spiritual light that we can regard as a reconfiguration of the light that he gave at the time of the Mystery of Golgotha; and the people of our time may place themselves into this light.

RUDOLF STEINER. London, May 2, 1913[16]

The Goetheanum. The School for Spiritual Science, 1919
(© Dokumentation am Goetheanu, Dornach)

Rudolf Steiner held the first lesson of the esoteric School of the Goetheanum, its First Class, on the evening of February 15, 1924, in the joinery workshop in Dornach. He began it with these words: "My dear friends, in this lesson I wish to give back to the School as esoteric institution the mission that in recent years it was in danger of being forcibly deprived of."[17]

These brief introductory words were resonant with meaning. The School for Spiritual Science had existed already *before* the Christmas Foundation Meeting, in the form of an esoteric institution. But in the period immediately preceding the Christmas Foundation Meeting this institution was becoming estranged from its mission, or at least there was a risk of this. Through the esoteric lessons that Steiner now initiated, the School was led back again into the proper sphere of its real task.

Steiner never stated exactly how long the School for Spiritual Science had existed as an esoteric institution. There are many indications that it was founded a long time before, possibly as early as 1910 and 1911. At this period the impulse for building a central location for spiritual-scientific work, a St. John's building at the center of the theosophical and anthroposophical movement, had not only assumed more tangible form but had acquired key importance. At the end of the eventful year of 1910, during which Steiner began to speak about the reappearance of Christ in the etheric,[18] and his first Mystery play, the drama of an esoteric community and its destiny,[19] was performed in Munich, he gave his Stuttgart lectures on occult history. There, in connection with the laying of the foundation stone for the anthroposophic branch group in Landhausstrasse, he first elaborated upon key aspects of the development of anthroposophic community and karmic factors at work in it.[20] Then, in the pre-Easter period of 1911, he spoke about occult physiology in Prague,[21] issuing an express invitation to anthroposophically oriented physicians to attend. Without doubt he wished them to be involved with him in methodically preparing spiritual-scientific work in a key domain of culture.[22] Shortly before St. John's tide 1911 he gave a spiritually seminal course on *The Spiritual Guidance of The Individual and Humanity*, which, at odds with his usual practice, he swiftly had typeset and published.[23]

At Michaelmas, in Neuchatel, he first spoke in detail about Christian Rosenkreutz, his initiation in the thirteenth century, and the beginning of the Rosicrucian movement—of incisive importance for Steiner's School impulse in the age of Michael.[24] Immediately after Neuchatel, he elaborated on the esoteric findings of his Rosicrucian research in relation to "The Etherization of the Blood," developing themes he had taken up in Prague in his *Occult Physiology*, and relating them to Christianity.[25] Then he travelled to Karslruhe, where, on October 4, he began the fundamental course *From Jesus to Christ*, which centered on the mystery secrets of the resurrection body.[26] As soon as the course ended, Steiner travelled to Stuttgart on October 15 to inaugurate the newly built branch premises in Landhausstrasse. At this festive event, Marie von Sivers suggested that pleasure at what had been achieved in Stuttgart ought not to push key plans for the St. John's building project into the background; and at the same time the first newsletter of the St. John's building association was published (dated October 15, 1911) and contained the following words by Steiner:

The idea of a *School for Spiritual Science is the necessary consequence that must be drawn from the spiritual knowledge* vouchsafed to our time. Today it is already possible, certainly, if we consider the colleagues working among us, to name teachers who, it appears, would be very willing to assume a teaching role. And only thereby, in fact, would spiritual science do justice to the task that was given it from the beginning: to make all domains of life fruitful. The School for Spiritual Science will take up the developmental potential of academic knowledge where its official proponents have allowed it to stagnate and rigidify, and lead it upward to a knowledge of the spirit, guiding it into the temple where its union with art and religion can give rise to living mystery.[27]

Rudolf Steiner's wording was surprising and highly remarkable—not only expressly stating the plan or intention for a School for Spiritual Science but placing this in a clearly Michaelic context, albeit without referring to this name. The "spiritual knowledge vouchsafed to our time" did however doubtless refer to the Michael age that had begun thirty-two years previously, in 1879. Rudolf Steiner referred to the idea of the School as a necessary consequence of the reality that had emerged in 1879 when Michael won a decisive victory over the ahrimanic hosts of the Spirits of Darkness.[28] ("This victory was a mighty breakthrough of the new, Michaelic light into the Earth's spiritual environment" [Sergei O. Prokofieff].[29])

The spirituality newly accessible to humankind under the aegis of the Archai Michael, the time spirit, needed to benefit civilization.[30] His further comments were likewise astonishing. Steiner spoke of future teachers at his planned School for Spiritual Science, and was thinking of very specific individuals in the theosophical–anthroposophical movement ("if we consider the colleagues working among us") with whom, clearly, initial discussions had already been held ("who, it appears, would be very willing to assume a teaching role"). Then Steiner stated that realization of this idea of a School had been central to the tasks of Anthroposophy from the out-set, and was really its intrinsic mission. This involved a wide-ranging influence on civilization in all fields of life. Indeed, Rudolf Steiner had spoken of this as early as 1902 in the first years of the movement he had initiated in Berlin and led from there.[31] He had never described or taught esoteric schooling as an end in itself but had always emphasized that love for one's fellow creatures and work accomplished for them in "selfless devotion and willingness for sacrifice" were the goals of spiri-tual development (*How to Know Higher Worlds*, 1905).[32]

As early as 1902 he had this socially relevant activity in view (with its aim of "creating new social forms" out of spiritual impulses) even if the beginning of the theosophical–anthroposophical movement had been very small and weak, and even on occasion cranky. ("It is not a matter of how much we achieve in one place or another in our first impetus, but whether we do the right thing, which is also determined by the karma of our era" [Apr. 19, 1903].[33])

As we saw, the passage on the School in the St. John's building association newsletter of October 15, 1911, ended with the following summary of its aims:

> The School for Spiritual Science will take up the develop-mental potential of academic knowledge where its official proponents have allowed it to stagnate and rigidify, and lead it upward to a knowledge of the spirit, guiding it into the temple where its union with art and religion can give rise to living mystery.

To those responsible for the St. John's building association, Rudolf Steiner had repeatedly stressed that the building
should *not* be a temple for Theosophy or Anthroposophy, a
sacred shrine of some kind, but a modern center of work, or
a place where modern culture could be pursued. It was a matter of transforming academic knowledge and certainly not of
devaluing or negating it: a place where it should be reborn
in a real sense. In other words, there should be a Michaelic
re-enlivening of dead or rigidified ideas (wherever they still
had developmental potential[34])—and these should be reunited
with art and religion in a new mystery center, the future locus
of a living mystery from which scientific, artistic and religious
impulses should permeate civilization.

⸺

On October 16, 1911, in Stuttgart, in an internal lecture
given one day after the inauguration of the branch house
in Stuttgart, and the date of publication of the newsletter
that spoke of the intention of a School for Spiritual Science,
Rudolf Steiner talked about the originating, Rosicrucian
impulses of the Theosophical Society and their later distortion. Here, indirectly, he clarified the spiritual continuity in
which further work should be accomplished, also in relation
to the School impulse (to which he did not explicitly refer).[35]
Only five weeks later he returned to Stuttgart and, in the
column hall in the basement of the branch building at Landhausstrasse, which has been established for esoteric and
ritual work, he announced the foundation of a Society for
Theosophical Life and Art and appointed certain individuals to their offices in this society "in the name of Christian
Rosenkreutz." One of the chief participants there, the painter
Imme von Eckardstein,[36] later looked back to this event as

one of "huge significance," a "moment of seriousness that made a deep impression" on her.

On December 15, 1911, at the delegates meeting of the annual general assembly of the German section of the Theosophical Society in Berlin (at the Architects' House in the Wilhelmsstrasse), Steiner gave a brief outline of the intentions underlying this foundation.[37] This was he said, an "attempt to found but not constitute a community of human beings" out of the world of spirit; to hearken to and follow a direct impulse of the spiritual world, whose point of departure was the being of Christian Rosenkreutz, who was also the protector of this foundation. The name Society for Theosophical Life and Art should, he said, be regarded as provisional only; and it would be altered no later than the point when this foundation, or the work it had initiated, should enter the *public* domain. But it was decisive for the whole undertaking that a new way of working should be established in accord with the will of the world of spirit, and that this should happen by means of a group of people working closely together. In their work and collaboration they should form a spiritual substance. All of those involved would accomplish their work autonomously and at their individual behest and yet do so in inner relationship to the others. Steiner said that he himself would represent the principles of the spiritual world in the Society for Theosophical Life and Art or interpret its intentions.[38]

In Berlin, Rudolf Steiner introduced the people who had so far been entrusted with offices by him, exclusively in the realm of art: Imme von Eckardstein would represent "theosophical art in general," Marie von Sivers would be responsible for literature, Adolf Arenson for music, Hermann Linde for painting, Felix Peipers for architecture, Alice Sprengel for

jewelry. In addition, Marie von Sivers was appointed cura-
tor of the whole foundation, supported by Carl Unger and
Sophie Stinde, who were both on the executive council of the
St. John's building association. Steiner emphasized that the
artistic realm was the first to be initiated or established in
this way because the people he named had in recent years
already undertaken the necessary active preparatory work
for this. Marie von Sivers, Imme von Eckardstein, Hermann
Linde and Adolf Arenson, at least, had already presented their
own works or artistic studies in line with Rosicrucian occult-
ism (Rudolf Steiner) and had been involved—either directly
or indirectly—not only in the mystery plays in Munich but
also in the building or design of branch premises in Berlin
and Stuttgart, and in Malsch. They were appointed, or took
on these responsibilities, because they had accomplished and
presented positive works, something that "already exists as a
reality in the world," as Steiner stressed. This was not, though,
he said, the award of some honor or accolade but the selfless
acceptance of responsibilities and duties, with "exclusion of
absolutely everything of a personal nature."

What Rudolf Steiner described here in a few words had
no doubt determined the obligatory ethic of the Rosicrucian
community for many centuries. The Rosicrucians had very
largely worked in secret, in deep modesty and hidden from
public view, without ambition and self-aggrandizement. Their
core tasks had included permeating ancient esoteric mystery
knowledge with the power of thought or spiritualized intelligence such that this mystery knowledge could enter civilization from the end of the nineteenth century, and be absorbed
by the scientific and academic world.[39] The Rosicrucians had
lived in anticipation of the age of Michael, and had prepared

for it. And the time had now come when their work could enter the public domain in a transformed way and in the light of Michael. In the realm of art a beginning should be made (or already had been with the mystery plays, the recitations, with buildings in the public view, and their interior design). But other fields, such as medicine and education, were doubtless intended to be added.

In general, in looking back to these days, it becomes apparent that the idea of the School described by Steiner in the first newsletter of the St. John's building association, the esoteric Rosicrucian impulse in the age of Michael, and the foundation of a Society for Theosophical Life and Art under the protection of Christian Rosenkreutz, were all closely related, or convergent, or were even an expression of one and the same initiative. There is evidence to suggest that those who were to take over teaching appointments in the planned School—some of whom had already given their agreement to this—were largely identical with those holding positions of responsibility in the Society for Theosophical Life and Art. But this means that the faculty or college appointed for the foundation and its society by Steiner was at the same time the directorate of the corresponding School area *in so far* as this had already so far taken shape.

From its inception in the hall of columns, with its ritual purposes, at Landhausstrasse, it had been clear to all those involved that the foundation and its society—and thus indirectly also the intended School—possessed an esoteric orientation. In addition, this was apparent from everything Steiner said in relation to it, and from the tone in which he spoke. But *because* this was an esoteric institution, he kept his utterances on the subject as brief as possible. Everything was only the seed of a seed, and yet also a spiritual reality oriented to the future. If we can say that Steiner's founding of the German section of the Theosophical Society in the fall of 1902 had been in response to a first call from the world of spirit,[40] then the founding of the Society for Theosophical Life and Art marked the beginning of a Rosicrucian–Michaelic School initiative as response to a second call, scarcely more than a decade after the beginning of theosophical–anthroposophical work, which (according to Steiner on Oct. 15, 1911) was intended to exert a transformative (fertilizing) influence on the various realms of life.

≈

The Rosicrucian orientation of Rudolf Steiner's work had met with great resistance within the Theosophical Society from the very outset. As early as 1907 he had felt compelled to detach his esoteric school from the context of this society (or at least from its Esoteric School).[41] The founding of the Society for Theosophical Life and Art likewise soon encountered severe hindrances. It is said that a member of the esoteric faculty appointed by Steiner was not psychologically capable of cultivating the required inner stance for this, at which Steiner halted the whole initiative, or at least did not continue with it, and henceforth spoke no more about it.[42] The details of what happened still remain unknown to this day, nor is it at all apparent whether the other individuals appointed by Steiner were aware of the scope of what the world of spirit was seeking to realize *through* Rudolf Steiner, and the whole context in which the new foundation and its society should have been working.

Although Steiner spoke no further about this initiative and (at least apparently) considered it closed, the prime movers in the St. John's building association continued to pursue the building and School impulse uninterrupted. This gave rise to a spiritually difficult situation, although Rudolf Steiner was probably the only one to recognize this. Over the next few years a building arose that was called the School of Spiritual Science (its *official* title from 1918 onward) but without a sustaining, esoterically—and thus truly—founded and united directorate. Steiner quite rightly wrote (in an *officially* published and also in this way intended) review of the history of the Goetheanum's development:

> Since Anthroposophy had already found scientifically trained members in the most varied fields during the period when work was begun on the building, so that there was a prospect of employing spiritual-scientific methods in these different disciplines, I was able to propose appending to the name of the building the phrase School for Spiritual Science.[43]

And yet in writing this he was only publicizing a part of what had been written in the first, largely internal newsletter of the St. John's building association in October 1911. At that time mention was made of the (both actual and potential) capacities of particular individuals in the anthroposophic movement, upon whom and on whose further development he was relying. Despite the failure of the Society for Theosophical Life and Art, this continued to be the case, and Rudolf Steiner continued to refer to the school of spiritual science after 1912, albeit sparingly and always in relation to the future. Thus in the city where he himself had studied, Vienna, in an internal course at Easter 1914 directly after Christian Morgenstern had passed away, he said:

> Just as Copernican texts remained on the Index of prohibited books right into the nineteenth century, so in a

sense the insights of spiritual science will long remain proscribed by other worldviews that are unable to detach themselves from the old prejudices of many centuries that have become ingrained habits of thinking. And the fact that this science of the spirit can, nevertheless, already reach hearts and minds, and is not beyond the pale of seekers in our time, can be shown by something that I will not flaunt but that may be mentioned as a sign of the fact that spiritual science speaks to something hidden in people's souls that is needed today.

We are already able in our time to build for this *science of the spirit a School* on Swiss soil. And, through the support of the friends of this spiritual movement and their understanding, we can indeed see its true symbol in the new architecture of the double-domed rotunda that is to rise from the heights of Dornach, near Basel, as a first monument to what this spiritual science must incorporate into modern culture. The fact that this building is already rising there, that the forms of its cupolas are already lifting above its circular structure, is something that now allows us to speak with far more hope and satisfaction of spiritual science, despite all the opposition, all the lack of understanding that it still inevitably encounters today in broad circles.[44]

Like few other colleagues and pupils of Rudolf Steiner, Christian Morgenstern had anticipated this building and possessed an astonishingly tangible premonition and real insight into its significance as a School of Spiritual Science on Swiss soil.[45]

World War I, with its destructive dynamic—also within human souls—made work on the St. John's building (later the Goetheanum) considerably more difficult, both outwardly and inwardly. And yet the physical building process advanced step by step through the hard work and commitment of those involved. The building, or the emerging institution, continued to bear its "additional name," the School for Spiritual Science, although Steiner scarcely ever mentioned it. In no lecture that year did he speak of the future intentions and spiritual background of the building, which he had at least intimated in October 1911. ("The idea of a School for Spiritual Science is the necessary consequence that must be drawn from the spiritual knowledge vouchsafed to our time.") Nor did he speak any further of the esotericism that should have been embedded in the initiative.

Eventually Rudolf Steiner took a positive or at least accepting stance toward the suggestion made to him that the building in Dornach should be inaugurated in the fall of 1920 with School courses that, alongside his own lectures, would largely include those of anthroposophically-oriented subject specialists who would demonstrate the stimulating or fertilizing power of Anthroposophy in various disciplines. The faculty members of the first Waldorf school in Stuttgart, carefully chosen and trained by him, had, since the fall of 1919, offered striking evidence of successful anthroposophic work and teaching in specific fields. Indeed these teachers at the Stuttgart Waldorf School were the people who most effectively supported him in the following years both at academic events and the School weeks with lectures that were predominantly their own, original work and testified to a high quality of research and teaching.[46]

In addition, during the first Dornach course for physicians in March and April 1920, and during an accompanying lecture course on Anthroposophy and diverse disciplines, anthroposophically oriented doctors and scientists, at least, had offered good contributions and talks. There were similar successes at the first meetings of other specialist fields, usually with the lively participation of the Stuttgart Waldorf teachers, who had academic caliber. In Oslo on December 2, 1921, Steiner said with much modesty and reticence:

> We have *tried* to establish the School for Spiritual Science in Dornach, Switzerland, the Goetheanum. We can say that *an attempt at least* has been made to fertilize the various scientific disciplines by complementing outstanding and important modern methods in medicine, science, sociology, history, and in the other very varied fields of human research, with what can be acquired through direct enquiry into the spiritual world itself. Here, specifically, *attempts* are being made also to offer practical suggestions for pedagogy through the Waldorf School in Stuttgart. *Attempts* have even been made to accomplish various things in the field of economics.[47]

At the end of 1921 Rudolf Steiner himself knew better than anyone that the work of anthroposophic lecturers remained inadequate, not to mention academic publications and monographs, or other scientific works and achievements. Yet he saw the good will of many and hoped that they would succeed in future in really deepening their work, and in extending and improving both the quality and quantity of their efforts. A place that aspired to the idea of the university (implicit in *Hochschule,* the German term for the School) needed to be involved in research, teaching, training, and to offer methodological stimulus in practical fields. In addition, it had to give evidence of, and publicize, scientific achievements if it were not to become the subject of public mockery.

In a crisis meeting in 1923, Rudolf Steiner said that the Goetheanum bore the additional name of a School for Spiritual Science, giving rise to expectations, or pretensions, that it would be scientifically and academically productive. If opponents were able to show that the Goetheanum was unable to produce scientific findings, then it was a lost cause: "We must approach the world honestly with things that have the potential to hold their own in science. We have to do that, don't we?"[48] Here Steiner was not speaking of the academic or scientific quality of his own work—of spiritual-scientific research in the narrower sense. From the very outset his concept of the School at Dornach included the forming of departments around this core research where people with qualifications in specific fields would work, and would enlarge their field with the help of newly emerging anthroposophic perspectives.

In the first course for physicians in Dornach, Steiner had not only outlined the principles of a spiritual-scientific physiology, pathology, and therapy but also opened up the prospect of very detailed doctorate themes and questions to be elaborated upon from these new perspectives, which he knew would offer important new insights.[49] He had likewise given a wealth of suggestions and specific proposals in other professional courses relating to science and social science. But by 1923 no one had pursued these suggestions. Nor had anyone undertaken to write a first textbook (which he also thought necessary) on spiritual-scientifically extended medicine; nor to revise and develop his scientific lectures as monographs offering new perspectives on heat and light; nor much else for which he hoped.[50]

Rudolf Steiner had not expected brilliant accomplishments worthy of the award of a Nobel Prize, but he had been looking for energetic, independent, and productive activity from people connected with him—who, however, mostly felt overtaxed by such demands and who, in part, did not really understand what he wanted of them, and what he was urgently hoping for. Not all anthroposophists took the idea and reality of the

School for Spiritual Science seriously. Some regarded Steiner himself as the embodiment, so to say, of this School, while others regarded it as mere phrase and largely thought of Dornach as a place for lectures and gatherings with an artistic emphasis. The majority did not realize how inadequately they had as yet accomplished the awaited and required transformation of their discipline. By the concept of *extending* (medicine and so on), Steiner did not mean an additive enlargement of each field and its existing professional know-how through the contents of Anthroposophy but a real transformation of its inner essence. He scarcely showed his great disappointment at many of the lectures that were held to mark the opening of the Goetheanum—during the first Dornach School course; and those speakers who were unable to critically scrutinize their own anthroposophic standards or that of their presentations, did not notice Steiner's dissatisfaction. He was truly pleased only with the artistic performances in the fall of 1920, even though there were also other isolated high points. In general, though, he considered that the first Dornach School course in 1920 had been something introduced [from without] "into this purely anthroposophical building."[51]

≈

Naturally things might and would improve in future, but time was passing—and the Goetheanum was not only the focus of criticism from journalists (and others) but also exposed to powers and forces bent on destroying it. Furthermore, Rudolf Steiner knew that the failure in 1911 and '12 to form an esoteric core had created a dangerous vacuum for the School idea. It seems very likely that, apart from him, there was no one living in Dornach between 1920 and 1923 who (amid all the activity) was really aware of what was lacking at the Goetheanum; this lack, except for Steiner's presence, left the building largely unprotected. An esoteric faculty under the protectorate of Christian Rosenkreutz that—starting with art—should have arisen but did not from 1911, would no doubt have been a protecting, sustaining, and helping power for the building and for the School impulse. In the fall of 1920, the Goetheanum had only been opened and in no way inaugurated, as Steiner made clear in personal conversations (and later in written form), *because* the conditions were simply not present for this inauguration.[52]

On New Year's Eve 1922/23, an arson attack destroyed the building entirely. This filled thousands of anthroposophists worldwide with fear, alarm, grief, and dismay, but it also took them completely by surprise. Steiner, however, was not surprised; he saw it coming and had warned about it for a long time in many different ways.[53] The Anthroposophical Society was not equal to the current state of the world, its events, and constellations of power, and, as an esoteric institution, the School for Spiritual Science had been sustained solely by Rudolf Steiner himself. *"An attempt was made to create the Goetheanum..., in a sense, in the image of other universities,"* he said after the Christmas Foundation Meeting in one of the esoteric lessons of the First Class.[54] He was referring indirectly to those colleagues who had not realized in the least that their compound mix of specialist knowledge and Anthroposophy,[55] combined with personal vanity and intellectualism, as well as a desire for social and academic recognition, was not a sustaining constituent of the founding in Dornach, but rather a real counter-force. The School for Spiritual Science as esoteric institution was at risk of being sundered from its mission, and paradoxically this threat came from within its own ranks.

> Before I myself took on leadership of the Anthroposphical Society, the impulse often arose to create something at the Goetheanum as independent university that, in a sense, was formed in the image of the external universities. This—and today it must be said—did not succeed. But it had to be undertaken as an experiment. We have had enough experiments now, and no more of them will be undertaken.[56]

≈

At the Christmas Foundation Meeting, Rudolf Steiner not only founded the Anthroposophical Society anew, but also its School: "...It is for this purpose that the School for Spiritual Science was founded at Christmas: so that esoteric life might once again infuse our Anthroposophical Society."[57] Steiner refounded the School as esoteric institution or esoteric school: *"This School for Spiritual Science at the Goetheanum will be...an esoteric school...."*[58] Why this new founding was necessary and why it was insufficient simply to clearly reformulate the developmental trajectory, the mission, and specific mode of working in the School, is not something Steiner mentioned at that time. Yet it was clear from his words that this was not just a change of course for an existing institution but a real, spiritual act of refounding. As always he was very precise and conscious in his formulations. The newly founded esoteric School would, he said, "emerge from the whole character of Anthroposophy" and "replace what was previously attempted as the so-called School for Spiritual Science, which cannot be regarded as having succeeded."[59]

During the Christmas Foundation Meeting, Steiner hinted at how spiritually serious the lack of success of the previous School had been—its distortion and estrangement from its real mission. He spoke of *"the grave transgressions of recent years"* and about what he hoped might be made good again in the near future.[60] Steiner rarely resorted to the idea of sin or transgression in his lectures and writings when describing human errors or failures. His use of the term in relation to processes at work at the Goetheanum in recent years was thus not only noteworthy, but also alarming in a certain sense. He spoke scarcely a word about the opponents and destroyers of the building throughout 1923, the year after it was burned down, but instead always questioned the state of the Anthroposophical Society, its lack of wakefulness and unity, its lack of courage, its lack of connection with the world at large, and its questionable inner identity.[61]

At the Christmas Foundation Meeting itself, Steiner put all this behind him and turned exclusively toward the new foundings (of both the Society and the School) and indeed toward the renewal of the whole anthroposophic movement.[62] At the Christmas Foundation Meeting, as previously quoted, he did however highlight indirectly the serious repercussions for the physical *and* spiritual being of the Goetheanum of the untrue, compromise-seeking, and pseudo-academic attitude of many in Dornach prior to 1923 and '24 in the context of School courses and elsewhere. But he moved on quickly from this and instead emphasized what should and *must* now acquire prominent importance: "A stronger impetus...is needed than has been employed in the past if the spirit that humanity needs is to enter our movement."[63]

Refounding the School, Steiner wished henceforth to place the Anthroposophical Society "at the service of the esoteric."[64] The esoteric School, as future core and soul of the Anthroposophical Society, was to show that it was possible to live tangibly with spiritual powers and forces; the School and those working in it would hearken to pure, originating impulses from the world of spirit, an undertaking whose preconditions Steiner had sought to lay down with the founding of 1911. He spoke of this at the Christmas Foundation Meeting:

> The proper impulse given to what should *henceforth* issue and emanate from Dornach must be...one that does not germinate on Earth but from the world of spirit. We will seek here to develop the strength to hearken to impulses from the spiritual world, and to pursue these.[65]

In Dornach, in future, instigated by the esoteric School, it would be vital that all involved in it (and indirectly also all members of the Anthroposophical Society) should feel themselves at every moment responsible toward the spiritual world—and to it *alone*. Awareness would develop that

> the spiritual world, at our present moment of historical development expects something of humanity, and this "something" applies in the most diverse fields of life. It is up to us to follow impulses from the spiritual world with clarity and truth.[66]

It was precisely in this sense and with this focus that those appointed to their offices or areas of responsibility through the founding in 1911 should have worked both together and individually to create an esoteric organ. However, in 1923/24, Steiner no longer spoke of the past, of failures or opportunities missed, but was looking only toward what, by hearkening to a third and last call from the world of spirit, should *henceforth* emerge. This was to come about first and foremost through the School as esoteric institution:

> Here in Dornach we must have a center in which it will be possible to speak of all important, direct experiences in the world of spirit to those who wish to hear this. This must be a place where strength is found not merely to point, in the intellectual, dialectical and empirical mode of modern science, to small signs of the spirit in one field or another. If Dornach is to fulfilll its mission it must be possible instead for people to listen with open minds to accounts of what occurs in the world of spirit, of the impulses originating there that enter natural existence and govern the natural world; of real experiences, actual powers, real beings in the spiritual world. The School of true spiritual science must be established here.... We can say that in Dornach people must be able to draw the strength really to look eye to eye with the spiritual world, in a spiritual sense, and to experience its realities.[67]

The mission of the School, in this sense, was to be esoteric, to really—and not just metaphorically—guide its members into the spiritual world: "And in the most rigorous sense, this should become the *content* of the School of Spiritual Science."[68]

Although Rudolf Steiner referred to the whole School as an esoteric one, and outlined its core task in these terms ("in the most rigorous sense"), he made clear at the same time that the School *department* of the General Anthroposophical Section would in particular be responsible for the (three classes of the) schooling path into the world of spirit: "First and foremost we have the general section, which will embody the esoteric aspect for all human souls."[69] At the same time, however, he stressed that, in contrast to previous tendencies, *all* professional and artistic activities in Dornach would be esoterically founded and sustained. What this means, though, is that Steiner did not in the least relinquish the university aspiration involving faculties for research, publication, teaching, and training, but stated, rather, that the School, as esoteric school, was distributed across these faculties or sections. The esoteric nature of the School or of the Goetheanum was nuanced according to different fields or departments;[70] but these latter, and the core of the work (in research, teaching, and training) would always be esoteric in nature. All the section leaders whom Steiner appointed at the Christmas Foundation Meeting—with the exception of Edith Maryon, who fell ill—were members of the esoteric faculty or executive council of the General Anthroposophical Society.

The leadership group of people around Rudolf Steiner was to become the central esoteric organ of the Goetheanum, and lead the General Anthroposophical Section of the School. At the same time, with each of the executive council members, Steiner wanted to develop and elaborate a specific field and represent its distinctive esoteric nature—the arts of speech and music with Marie Steiner-von Sivers, medicine (including curative education) with Ita Wegman, the plastic arts with Edith Maryon, the fine arts with Albert Steffen, the sciences with Guenther Wachsmuth, and mathematics and astronomy with Elisabeth Vreede.

As he had already done in 1911, when he founded the Society for Theosophical Life and Art, Steiner made it clear that these appointments, and thus the establishing of School sections themselves, accorded with the previous work and accomplishments of particular individuals: "We will not proceed in an abstract way here but instead, drawing on existing spheres of activity, will compose and establish the sections from these realities, based on what is already there."[71] He did not speak during the Christmas Foundation Meeting about the necessary inner, moral stance in relation to these responsibilities—which, again, he did not regard as honors and accolades but as an obligation that each person undertook. He may, however, have spoken of this at the internal meeting when the council was constituted, although no reliable documentation exists of this. It is unclear whether Steiner connected the work of the esoteric executive organ with any kind of pledge from each member;[72] no such undertaking is recorded in the written memoirs of those involved. It was nevertheless clear that the functional capacity of this group was decisive for the success and the ongoing esoteric and exoteric survival of the Goetheanum and its School for Spiritual Science.

﹌

As a newly founded esoteric school, the School was to form a "bedrock for Anthroposophy" within civilization,[73] and to exert a clarifying and intensifying effect within the General Anthroposophical Society. The Anthroposophical Society was to be regenerated, and all half-hearted compromise, unclear or diplomatic stances toward Anthroposophy overcome among the ranks of School members. In no uncertain terms Rudolf Steiner said to those who applied to join the esoteric School and were admitted to it: "The fact is that laxness has entered the Anthroposophical Society to a very great degree in recent years. To ensure this is dispelled again will be the task, one of the tasks, that falls to members of this School."[74]

The seriousness that should become intrinsic to the whole anthroposophic movement must, he said, come to expression in future in particular in its esoteric school. Absolute, sacred, but also active seriousness must emanate from the esoteric School, thus gradually permeating the whole anthroposophic movement, and with it also the Anthroposophical Society.[75] In no way did Rudolf Steiner intend this *seriousness* to mean a stance of moral gravity or simply conduct of a strict, correct kind, but primarily a phenomenon of awakened consciousness. As he said to School members of the First Class in September 1924, there was far too little seriousness in anthroposophic circles for what "is actually flowing through the anthroposophic movement";[76] for this reason, at least in members of the esoteric School, a core of people should develop who—based on their knowledge and awareness (i.e., their insight)—could possess or develop an appropriate stance toward Anthroposophy and the spiritual mission of the Goetheanum.[77] Among key characteristics and virtues that Rudolf Steiner counted on in School members was their willingness, indeed their will, for absolute truthfulness. In an esoteric lesson, he said to them:

> We should feel responsible right down to the very words we utter; above all, this sense of responsibility should extend to us scrutinizing in the most serious way whether every word we speak is something we can stand up for as the truth. You see, statements that are not true, even if they proceed from, if you like, good will, are something that act destructively within an esoteric movement. We must harbor no illusions on this score; we must be absolutely clear about this. Our intentions are not the important issue, for people frequently take these very lightly. What counts, however, is whether what we speak is effective truth. One of the first duties of an esoteric student is that he not only feels obliged to say what he believes to be true, but to examine whether what he says is really the objective truth. Only if, through objective

truth, we serve the divine, spiritual powers whose forces infuse this School will we be able to navigate our way through all the difficulties that will place themselves in Anthroposophy's path.[78]

Soon after the new esoteric School of the Goetheanum was established, Steiner made clear to its pupils that divine, spiritual powers infused it. He frequently reiterated that *he himself had not* actually refounded this esoteric School as such, but that he had only done it on behalf of these divine, spiritual powers as their representative. The School, he said, had been constituted directly "through the will of the world of spirit itself."[79] Nor had it been really founded on Earth at all, within earthly conditions—whether in Dornach or any other earthly place—but rather in the suprasensory worlds. All the rest was merely an earthly reflection, the "earthly image of something spiritually established." "The world of spirit had itself in a sense to reveal the will to create such a School."[80] Earthly occurrences within space and time in the esoteric School were, he said, the body of something that flows from the life of spirit: "And thus everything that happens in such a School is the outward expression of activity that actually occurs in the suprasensory world of spirit."[81]

Two months after the School began, in a Class Lesson on Good Friday, 1924, Steiner said that he had "drawn this resolve from the spiritual world."[82] He gave no further information about this, saying only, some time later: "This School has been spiritually instituted; it arose after I hearkened to what the spiritual powers governing the world regard as the right thing specifically for our age."[83] Steiner did not reveal in this esoteric lesson what situation had led him to turn to the world of spirit; but it was hard to overlook the fact that this was connected with the crisis in which humanity found itself *as well as* with the catastrophic situation of the Goetheanum. The esoteric School of the Goetheanum, he said already in the early lessons, was "instituted by the spiritual world for the present time"[84] and "intended by it in full seriousness."[85] It had been given "out of the spirit, out of the life of spirit that was revealing itself to our present age" (Feb. 15, 1924),[86] and had arisen "by the will of the spiritual powers that *today* govern the world" (Apr. 11, 1924).[87]

At this stage, Rudolf Steiner did not yet speak the name *Michael* in the context of the First Class; members of the School did not learn that it was in fact a Michaelic Rosicrucian school until many months later.[88] Only then did Steiner speak expressly of what had nonetheless been implicit from the beginning. Founded as "instituted by the world of spirit *for the present age,*" by the will of the "spiritual powers *today* governing the world," the Dornach School at and after the Christmas Foundation Meeting had a special relationship to Michael, the prevailing spirit of the times—the spirit whose counsel and resolve Rudolf Steiner had asked for at a very difficult moment.

> Thus it has only been possible to found this esoteric School by eliciting the will that…since the last third of the nineteenth century, really guides and leads human spiritual concerns: the Michael will. (Sept. 20, 1924)[89]

2

The Michael School and the First Class

If you hold the Class lessons, wherever it may be, always remember that what you are doing is not delivering a scholarly lecture but standing within a cultus, or enactment; that you must accomplish an enactment that can connect us with the mystery stream of all ages.

RUDOLF STEINER, March 3, 1925[90]

In time and eternity be
A pupil in the light of Michael
In the love of gods
In the cosmic heights.

From a mantra by Rudolf Steiner for Ita Wegman
(© Ita Wegman Archive, Arlesheim)

On August 2, 1924, in the nineteenth Class lesson in Dornach at the end of his path through the sequence of teachings that he had been developing for more than six months, beginning February 15, Steiner surprised his listeners:

> As you have heard in the general lectures on Anthroposophy, such inner teachings of the heart first resounded in Michael's suprasensory School. At that time, the beginning of the nineteenth century, they were mighty pictures in the imaginative cultus, in which revelations of the school from the fifteenth, sixteenth, and seventeenth centuries were presented before souls chosen to be in the proximity of Michael. These revelations were conducted, in the specific meaning of the word, by Michael himself and his hosts. Now we stand before this anthroposophic School founded by Michael. We feel that we are within it. Michaelic words should therefore characterize the path that leads us into the world of spirit and the human "I"—Michaelic words. These Michaelic words of the esoteric Michael School formed, we can say, the first stage of the classes.[91]

Seven months previously Steiner had spoken of the necessary esoteric character that henceforth should infuse the anthroposophic movement. ("Only by this means will it be possible to give the anthroposophic movement its real spiritual content."[92]) This *real spiritual content* was what Steiner then proceeded to give to the community of anthroposophists during the course of 1924, despite the fact that the preconditions for this as he described them (in the sense of an esoteric character permeating and determining the General Anthroposophical Society) had not yet really happened.[93] He did this, however, with the facilitating, future-oriented, trusting, and unconditionally positive gesture that was characteristic of him.[94] Steiner offered this spiritual content in the esoteric Class lessons, and also in the accompanying karma lectures and the *Leading Thoughts* published at the same time.[95] The first Class Lesson was held in the joinery workshop at the Goetheanum on Friday evening, February 15 1924, at 8.30 p.m. At the same place and time, one day later, he delivered the first lecture in the cycle of karma presentations. The spiritual culmination and core of this course was reached only shortly after St. John's Tide, 1924, after long and careful preparation. At this point, Steiner's accounts began to engage with the cosmic, suprasensory destiny of the Michael community; *"Thus souls were prepared who then descended into the physical world, and who, through all these preparations should receive the impulse to approach everything that was then to act on Earth as Anthroposophy..."* [96]

Only very late in the course of the karma lectures did it thus become apparent to some anthroposophists that Steiner was in fact revealing to the anthroposophical community its own destiny—that is, its spiritual antecedents and mission in a far more precise and detailed way than he had done previously in occasional intimations. His account, "World History in the Light of Anthroposophy," which he had elaborated upon in the evening lectures of the Christmas Foundation Meeting (and similarly his reflections on occult history in the Holy Nights of 1910/11) were met with scarcely any understanding of their importance for the origins, history, and challenges facing the anthroposophic movement and the Society.[97] Notwithstanding this, Rudolf Steiner carried on, as ever hoping and expecting his pupils and colleagues to awaken spiritually—that is, he was relying on the Michaelites' self-knowledge, both individually and as members of a great, significant community.

In the karma lectures of summer 1924, he described the development of this community and the preparations lasting almost two millennia for fulfillling their anthroposophic tasks in the twentieth century. From the summer onward, in the few weeks remaining to him before he was forced to take to his sickbed, he also clearly related the Class lessons to the processes at work in the Michael School and to its contents.

≈

In his lectures on karma, Rudolf Steiner did not elaborate on the beginning of the actual community around Michael or the connection between this leading archangel of the Sun and the beings of the third hierarchy united with him and numerous human souls and elemental beings. However, he did outline the situation of this real Michael community at the time of Christ, describing how Michael and his hosts—his garment of rays—experienced the Christ spirit's departure from the Sun sphere, the cosmic world heart: the loss of his being. Steiner described this as a mighty, profound, and shattering experience for the community around Michael, and in relation to the human souls involved, he said:

> This is...one of the events that we must consider: that the human souls connected with the anthroposophic movement bear within them this sense and vision: "We are united with Michael on the Sun; the Christ, who hitherto has sent his impulses from the Sun to Earth, now departs from the Sun to unite with earthly evolution!"[98]

These human souls also included the individualities who (as described at the Christmas Foundation Meeting and also in Stuttgart in 1910 and '11) had in previous centuries been incarnated as Eabani and Gilgamesh, Cratylus and Mysa, and

Aristoteles and Alexander: the latter most recently in order to introduce into earthly civilization significant, future-oriented impulses in the period immediately preceding that of Christ.[99]

The departure of Christ from the Sun sphere and his turn toward the Earth, his path "from the light-filled heights of the Sun kingdom into the darkness of Earth,"[100] led Michael also to make extensive sacrifices. He, whose gaze had been directed to humanity "from the very outset,"[101] and who, already *prior* to Golgotha, had been very much involved in the sacrificial paths of Christ and the Nathan soul,[102] now resolved to send toward Earth and thus to release or emancipate the world thoughts of cosmic intelligence that hitherto he had kept in his responsibility and administered.

> He [Michael] was the most illustrious among the archangels inhabiting the Sun. He was the spirit who not only transmitted the physical-etheric sun rays but with these also dispatched to Earth an inspiring intellectuality.[103]

In this way, with the living light of worlds of the spirit's cosmic thoughts, Michael had inspired spiritual life in the mystery centers over many centuries. Back in the last pre-Christian Michael era, a thinker such as Aristotle had already experienced this, and propounded it, as an inner activity of intelligence that marked the beginning of the emancipation of earthly from cosmic intelligence, or an anticipation of what would eventually become distinctive of modern spiritual life and thus also of the life of thought.

Following the Mystery of Golgotha,[104] Michael then resolved to entirely release cosmic intelligence and allow it to stream down as a sacred rain to Earth, the planet of Christ, on whose further destiny not only humanity's future but also to a large degree that of the cosmos would depend.[105] According to

Steiner, the sacred rain, the emancipation of intelligence from the sun sphere and its incorporation into the human, was a process that took over a millennium. Only with the conclusion of this evolutionary period did the rays of intelligence arrive fully on Earth, to become the human being's "personal-individual intelligence":

> Within the choir of the archangels in the sun region there resounded from Michael's being the mighty words, *"The power of my realm that I administered here is no longer here; it must stream, surge, and flow further upon the Earth below!"*[106]

In the process thus initiated here, which would determine the further history of human consciousness and culture, outstanding members of the Michael community became active, engaging with it in full responsibility. As Rudolf Steiner described, key incarnation tasks arose for them on Earth soon after the end of the first post-Christian millennium. In the evolution of the human mind after the final arrival of what had formerly been cosmic intelligence and its transformation into a personal, individual intelligence, they needed to ensure that the cosmic origins of human intelligence, or thoughts themselves, should not be forgotten entirely. Furthermore, humanity needed increasingly to take responsibility for the processes at work in intelligence, that is, to practice responsibly independent thinking, and connect this with the "I," the individual core of human nature, awareness of which was continually unfolding alongside these processes.

Members of the Michael community belonging to the Platonic stream, those who founded and led, among other things, the School of Chartres, were, said Steiner, engaging primarily with the first task. At the beginning of the second post-Christian millennium they not only represented a Christianized Platonism, which they disseminated in the form of imaginative pictures of the world and of human evolution, but at the same time also taught a way of handling intelligence that preserved and emphasized its cosmic origin.[107] The Dominicans, who succeeded them and whose work was attuned to that of the Platonists with a jointly composed quality of wisdom inherent in the Michael impulse, fought by contrast for acknowledgement of the human "I" as an entity of active and responsible thinking. Fighting against the anti-individualizing tendency toward abstraction and formalization, they endeavored to assert the objective reality of the nature of thinking. *"It was a thin spirituality that was saved here, but spirituality nevertheless." "The whole of Scholasticism is a human struggle for clarity about the influx of intelligence... of light-filled, spiritual intelligence."*[108]

According to Steiner, the common task of the Platonists (the School of Chartres and the Cistercian Order) and the Aristotelians, who formed the core of the Dominican community, was to develop the human being's earthly engagement with intelligence, and this intelligence itself, in a way that would enable Michael to re-unite with it in the period of his regency beginning at the end of the nineteenth century. This time, though, he would do so not in the cosmic realm of the Sun, but on Earth, and in the free heart of the human being, for which Michael "is preparing light":

[Michael] frees thoughts from the realm of the head; he opens their way to the heart; he kindles enthusiasm from human sensibility so that a person can live in soul devotion to everything that can be experienced in *the light of thought.*[109]

≈

Michael sent cosmic intelligence to Earth following the descent there of Christ, and made it available to the greatest degree to the self-emancipating human being, unprotected by safeguarding mystery centers. And he was fully aware of the attendant dangers. According to Rudolf Steiner, he knew that in the many centuries until the next era of his regency, fateful things might happen in earthly engagement with the forces of intelligence; and yet he had no other choice. In this situation, the Platonist and Aristotelian members of his community did their utmost to maintain connection between the human spirit and the spirit in the cosmos. Alongside the work of the Dominicans, the community around Christian Rosenkreutz also initiated its spiritual work on Earth. The Rosicrucians, too, wished to work actively on behalf of Michael to prepare his future influence on Earth, and in the subsequent centuries they did this in a hidden yet extremely effective way.[110]

Michael himself *in heavenly loneliness*, said Steiner, gave lessons from the beginning of the fifteenth century. Without a tangible means of working on Earth, he instructed those belonging to his community—including the human souls who had recently united with him in the Sun sphere, who at this point had detached themselves again from their Orders, or excarnated—in lessons lasting centuries that would be of outstanding importance for their future work on Earth. In a love that encompassed cosmic sun space, Michael completed the next steps in the forming of spiritual community, with an orientation toward a common spiritual content. He taught anthroposophic and cosmosophic connections, mysteries of the human being and the cosmos in, Steiner said, "wondrously grandiose teachings," in "great, mighty, universal words" that penetrated the community as *inner teachings of the heart.* He brought vividly to life for the community "what had once lived as Michael wisdom in the Sun mysteries."[111] In other words he unfolded the "great teachings of the ancient mysteries" in an encompassing panorama. But it was by no means a matter just of recollected repetition, gathering and concentration of past truths, but of their transformation toward the future. In the suprasensory Michael School there was an aim toward the future, "toward what should become the new mysteries."[112] The ancient mysteries were to be transformed into the new through the Christ impulse, which had been active in the world since the turning point of time and the Mystery of Golgotha.

As Sergei O. Prokofieff puts it, this involved "true understanding of the cosmic being of the Christ and his deed at the Mystery of Golgotha."[113] With his instruction, Michael was not only cultivating a community-building or consolidating spirit-remembering among the Michaelites (who in former times, either when incarnated or excarnated, had approached closely to this inner content now taught in concentrated, condensed and summarized form), but at the same time was also preparing the transition of spiritual contents into that intelligent consciousness that in the dawning age of the consciousness soul would be *the* decisive quality and precondition for Michaelic activity on Earth.

"Everything [in the Michael School] was taught from the point of view that the Michaelic must now be developed in a different way in human evolution below on Earth, through the human soul's own intelligence."[114] Not only the School's contents as such offered testimony in this way of the development of mystery culture or of the transformation of the old into the new mysteries, but the whole mode of instruction was also marked by the character of the new age that was dawning. The mysteries of the future would be those of the awakened, thinking "I" that would be able to find new access to Christ–Michael in and with its spiritualized intelligence. It was precisely in this sense that the members of the Rosicrucian community were working, within the limits of their earthly possibilities: "This was the work of the Rosicrucians: to shape the wisdom of the primordial world in a way that could gradually adapt it to the modern spirit and the modern soul."[115]

Teaching in the Michael community was not an end in itself but had a definite goal—one also circumscribed in temporal terms: it offered a "mighty prospect of what was to happen."[116] According to Steiner, Michael taught "what is to happen when the new Michael age begins," or in other words he was preparing the arrival of his next earthly age of influence in the last third of the nineteenth century. His colleagues and pupils received compelling exhortations whose aim was *"to ensure that those surrounding Michael might [in future] plunge in to the Michael stream, and take up the impulses that can once again unite intelligence with the being of Michael."*[117]

Steiner's use of the word *plunge* here indicates the drama connected with this prospect, and with the mission clearly required of members of the Michael community at the beginning, already, of the new age. The changes that occurred on Earth with the arrival there of an originally cosmic intelligence were highly dynamic and full of consequence at this point already. At the beginning of the fifteenth century, the members of this community witnessed from the Sun sphere how the beings of the first hierarchy were conducting earthly powers of intelligence fully into the human being's neurosensory system—a process that Steiner described as one "surrounded by mighty storms of thunder and lightning" in the cosmic perception of the Michaelites.[118]

What was thus accomplished on Earth, in world evolution, and *had* to be accomplished to make possible the dawning of the age of the consciousness soul, was a far-reaching reconfiguration of the human constitution with an accelerated further development of the neurosensory system, which only now took up its leading position in the human organism.[119] The human being on Earth now became a head thinker and was no longer centrally organized around the heart; he acquired both the organic-physical and functional capacities to employ the full scope of the forces of intelligence in future, and to do so in the manner and direction he himself desired, which in no way excluded using intelligence to realize evil. In this context, Michael and his hosts also perceived how, from the fifteenth century onward, a spiritual counter-school was established in the depths of the Earth as a reaction to their Sun school or its future-preparing instruction.

As Rudolf Steiner described this in his karma lectures in the summer of 1924, an intense resistance by ahrimanic power on Earth was activated to counter the mighty spread of the cosmic Michael School: "...*[the Michael School] was something huge, something that profoundly alarmed the ahrimanic demons on Earth, precisely in the fifteenth, sixteenth, and seventeenth centuries and into the eighteenth. It awoke terrible consternation in them.*"[120] Established by Ahriman and his hosts in the depths of the Earth, the counter-school's impulses ascended with "demonic spiritual vapors" and aimed increasingly to encompass human forces of intelligence and take full possession of them. Not only was Ahriman preparing to prevent Michael from being able to reunite human head intelligence with heart processes—and thus with the whole human entity and also with himself—from the nineteenth century onward, but he also wished to sunder intelligence from Michael for all times and absorb it into his own being. Of this Rudolf Steiner said:

> At the same time as intelligence sank down to Earth from the cosmos, the ahrimanic powers continually increased their aspirations to sunder this cosmic intelligence from Michael as it became earthly, and to realize it on Earth alone in a Michael-free condition. This was the great crisis of the beginning of the fifteenth century through to today, the crisis in which we still stand, the crisis that comes to expression as the battle of Ahriman against Michael: Ahriman who employs everything at his disposal to contest Michael's dominion over the intelligence that had now become earthly....[121]

> To be an anthroposophist means, among other things: to understand this battle, at least to some degree.[122]

Rudolf Steiner hinted at the developing willingness of the pupils of Michael to plunge in to this conflict in future and to unite their own destiny with its outcome. In the suprasensory Michael School between the fifteenth and eighteenth centuries, a real "urge toward Anthroposophy" was implanted in the Sun sphere[123] along with a willingness to work wholeheartedly on Earth for this Michael-dedicated Anthroposophy from the end of the nineteenth century, that is, from the dawn of the new Michael age. Suprasensory teaching in the spiritual realm of the Sun, and the "magnificent and truly bountiful retrospect upon the ancient mysteries" that were to provide the "spiritual point of departure for founding new mysteries of the present and future,"[124] took place far from the Earth but not unrelated to it. The Michaelites experienced, rather, what was unfolding and being prepared within the sphere of Earth, and were already involved and concerned with the consequences of these earthly events in the suprasensory Michael School. From the spiritual sphere they also followed with great attention and active participation the Rosicrucians' sacrificial rites in the second half of the fifteenth century,[125] the swift advances of scientific materialism in the sixteenth century, and the occult conference of the Rosicrucians that, at the beginning of the seventeenth century—in a situation that was already extraordinarily difficult—led to a saving intervention in the planetary sphere.[126,127]

Finally, shortly before being reincarnated and the incipient earthly conflict with Ahriman over spiritualization of intelligence, members of the community experienced a considerable strengthening, especially in a social regard. No longer in the far-distant Sun sphere, but already in the closer vicinity of Earth—in a realm *immediately adjoining* the physical, sensory world,[128] a great, comprehensive event occurred in the spiritual world in the first decades of the nineteenth century, when the actual conflict was set to begin. Rudolf Steiner described this specifically as a heavenly rite, the culmination in certain respects of previous instruction in the Michael School. In its ritual enactments, this cultus concluded and encompassed, in a realm close to the Earth, what had occurred in solar realms between the fifteenth and eighteenth centuries. Here the content of the teachings of the Michael School first acquired imaginative, ritual form. In a cosmic, spiritual festival, suprasensory acts of worship were performed, a mighty elaboration of images of spiritual life, of cosmic entities, those of the hierarchies, in connection with the great, cosmic ether influences and with the effects of human actions on Earth....[129]

Michael was certainly no longer giving instruction here; instead his circle of pupils and collaborators, foremost among them leading Platonists and Aristotelians, now by their own impulse and responsibility, as a spiritual deed, allowed the teachings of the Michael School received in previous centuries to resurface and reawaken in *jointly woven* cosmic Imaginations. The rites configured from these cosmic Imaginations, and celebrated and experienced together by leading Michaelites, decisively consolidated the unity and resolve of each member of the community to work together: "Those who today feel the urge *to unite in the Anthroposophical Society*, were gathered together at the beginning of the nineteenth century in suprasensory regions to accomplish that mighty cultus of Imaginations."[130]

As materialism was culminating on Earth in the first decades of the nineteenth century, therefore—leading to the worst consequences for the Earth's etheric environment, where the Mystery of Golgotha would be repeated in etheric form[131]—the Michaelites, in the accomplishment of a shared ritual enactment, gained courage and strength for their mission. More than ever they regarded themselves as a community, and from their ranks was to emerge, from the beginning of the twentieth century, the Anthroposophical Society or, rather, its inner, esoteric core. In certain respects, therefore, the Michael cultus was the Pentecost conclusion to a process of developing community that had been in preparation in cosmic heights for almost two millennia. Henceforth the Michaelites, having incarnated on Earth, were to develop the power of initiative and together carry Anthroposophy into civilization, facing all obstacles and willing to meet existential risks. Sergei O. Pro- kofieff wrote:

> In relation to the [Michael] cultus, Rudolf Steiner indi- cated...that what participants in the Michael School absorbed in a more cognitive fashion, now united with their will in ritual enactment; that is, it became a source of their spiritual initiative. From then on, as pupils of Michael, they not only wished to acquire suprasensory knowledge but draw upon this to work on Earth in accord with a *renewal of the Pentecost event*.[132]

In the suprasensory Michael School between the fifteenth and eighteenth centuries, a foundation was laid for the new mysteries, thus accomplishing a transition from the era of the Father to that of the Son. The suprasensory cultus subse- quently facilitated the "further transition from the Son to the Spirit...and thus to the capacity to work on Earth out of a spiritual impulse."[133]

≈

Looking back with awareness of these contexts, it is not dif- ficult to see that, soon after the twentieth century began, Rudolf Steiner gathered around him the souls connected with him and the Michael impulse.[134] Through his lectures and their content he sought to awaken a spirit remembering, pur- suing various paths to accomplish this.[135] At the end of 1910, after seven years of preparing the ground through his teach- ing and lecturing work, Steiner began to reveal certain details of destiny connections among the anthroposophic community (and in Stuttgart gave the course entitled *Occult History*). Performances of the mystery plays and—especially—the building project in Dornach, were also connected with the core mission of the Michael community, and were at the same time an aid for all involved in it to gradually awaken to their destined tasks.[136] There is no doubt that the building's forms, as well as its sculptural motifs and paintings, displayed many elements that were intimately related to the Michael mysteries and the suprasensory teachings of the fifteenth to the eighteenth centuries. The Christ-permeated anthropology and cosmology of the Michael School acquired visible form in the St. John's building (or Goetheanum): they were presented *tangibly* again to the community less than a hundred years after its experience of the Michael cultus in which participants witnessed powerful cosmic Imaginations ("a mighty elaboration of images of spiritual life, of cosmic entities, of the hierarchies").

In his address at the laying of the foundation stone for the Dornach building, which was to form the center of the School for Spiritual Science. Steiner made very clear on September 20, 1913, what spiritual hopes and tasks, of world-historical proportions, were connected with the planned building.[137] From May 1913 he had given his first great Michael lectures (in London and Stuttgart) and made unceasing efforts to ensure that members of the Anthroposophical Society should recognize their key communal mission in the twentieth century in developing an influential School for Spiritual Science based on a spiritualization of thinking: "O Man, know thyself… "[138]

But in the following years not a great deal occurred among those connected with Rudolf Steiner. The world war intervened in central Europe's history, and the situation in the subsequent postwar period was informed by great tensions and destructive elements that created further obstacles to both outer and inner work. On January 1, 1924, at the end of the Christmas Foundation Meeting—Steiner's last great effort to awaken the Michaelites and nurture their common initiative and activity—he said:[139]

> If we look out today into the world, we find a huge potential for destruction that has already existed for years now. Powers are at work that give us an intimation of the kinds of abyss into which Western civilization is still to plunge.

He stated categorically that the essence of Anthroposophy and the Michael mission was still slumbering or dreaming "in the deepest chambers of the heart" of most anthroposophists, in the form of an unconscious secret, and that the Michaelites must now quickly begin "to engage their hearts strongly" and to work in communal resolve with "inner, sacred zeal."[140] The people connected with Rudolf Steiner, the suprasensory school of Michael and the Michael cultus should, he hoped, become helpers of Michael in "conquering the intelligence that has fallen from heaven to Earth," and in the necessary battle with Ahriman: "more than any other battle, this one is located in the human heart." "*Michael needs hosts of helpers....*"[141]

Steiner then took one last step forward with the etheric foundation stone laid in the hearts of members, his esoteric Class lessons and the karma lectures. He now had (whether he wished or no[142]) to reveal, unsparingly, what had for a long time stood in the background of his lectures: for the first time he spoke unmistakably not only about the esoteric background and spiritual mission of the Anthroposophical Society within civilization, but about its current configuration and possible development. In this connection he also explained that at the beginning of the twentieth century—unlike the situation a millennium previously—the souls of the Michael community he called Aristotelian had to incarnate *first* in order to clear a way for Anthroposophy in the spiritual conflicts of the modern era: "First of all those who had, more or less, worked as Aristotelians had to descend once more, since, under the influence of intellectualism the time had not yet come when spirituality could be deepened again."[143] If their work should succeed to a certain degree, thus creating conditions in central Europe for the work of Anthroposophy to continue—in the public domain, based on a School for Spiritual Science and with associated centers of work and activity in many places—then, from the end of the twentieth century the Platonist-oriented Michaelites could unite with the quickly reincarnating Aristotelians to pursue common endeavors on Earth for the future.[144]

In this context, the schooling course of the First Class—the esoteric school of the Goetheanum—had a fundamental importance. Here, according to Steiner, it was a matter of being face to face with the world of spirit, that is, in intimate directness and immediacy. In the twentieth century even the Michaelites were in danger not only of failing in their historical mission but losing their thinking power in the ahrimanic stream of destruction. They had to perceive and acknowledge themselves and their situation in space and time, and finally awaken to their own individuality, their destined tasks, and those of their community. The path of the esoteric Class lessons from earthly "I"-consciousness to the higher and true "I"[145] was at the same time the path to this awakening in the suprasensory sphere. The First Class mediated the capacity and strength to survive and exist there. Class lessons took their point of departure directly from the sphere of evil, of Ahriman and the second crucifixion of Christ in the etheric as consequence of a materialistic darkening of the ether world during the nineteenth century.[146] But this means that they began directly with the Michaelic–ahrimanic conflict in this era. In his karma lectures, in connection with an account of the suprasensory school of Michael, Steiner said:

> This was the great crisis of the beginning of the fifteenth century through to today, the crisis in which we still stand, the crisis that comes to expression as the battle of Ahriman against Michael: Ahriman who employs everything at his disposal to contest Michael's dominion over the intelligence that had now become earthly.... To be an anthroposophist means, among other things to understand this battle, at least to some degree.

Henceforth it became apparent that membership of the esoteric school at the Goetheanum implied, from the Christmas Foundation Meeting onward, that one not only understood this battle but was a *jointly responsible participant in it*. The fact that members of the esoteric school now assumed responsibility for representing Anthroposophy in the world demanded of them, as Steiner made clear, a willingness to take upon themselves all the difficulties associated with this conflict. They could no longer be merely listening or even understanding anthroposophists. Instead they must now firmly resolve to realize the common will that, in the face of the whole ahrimanic threat, had once again been emphatically affirmed in the Michael cultus:

> I am here as a representative of the Anthroposophy that issues from the Goetheanum.[147]

> You shall still be tested in your courage to avow the voice
> that you can well hear through the inclination of your
> mind and soul, through the inclination of your heart.[148]

Among members of the Anthroposophical Society there
was a widespread longing of the heart for Anthroposophy
and its esoteric core—and they took up the spiritual contents
of the Christmas Foundation Meeting with as much enthusiasm as the mantras of the First Class.[149] But they found it
much harder to lead their experience of the dimension of
inwardness into strong, efficacious action, and to let the lofty
spirituality of real fire powers in the heart sphere become
deeds for civilization.

Nevertheless, Rudolf Steiner continued to rely on the ultimate success of this process. At the end of May 1924, after the
fourteenth Class lesson—which required of pupils an inner
decision to embark upon the Christ path into the world of
spirit—and in which the true "I" began to resound through
the higher "I" ("Not I but Christ in my 'I'"[150]) he told them
for the first time in all clarity what kind of school they were
actually in: "This esoteric School is the true Michael School;
it is the institution of those spiritual beings who possess the
direct Inspiration of the cosmic will of Michael."[151]

Lesson 14 speaks of Christ, Lucifer, Ahriman, and their
activity—their real voice in the human heart. The Michael
School taught the Michaelic path toward Christ and the true
"I"—albeit with all attendant dangers and afflictions that
were and remain intrinsic to the history of the twentieth century and forthcoming times. In this context, it appears apt
and necessary that the spiritual identity of the School was
revealed at the moment when the sphere of Christ's battle
with adversarial powers for the human heart—as the organ

of Christ–Michael and decisive locus of the spiritualization of intelligence (and its reuniting with Michael)[152]—was incorporated into the sequence of the esoteric lessons. But Steiner expressed this even more clearly in the subsequent period, after speaking, in the karma lectures in July, about the suprasensory Michael School and the Michael cultus. At the end of lesson 19, and thus of the whole course, or its first section, he spoke expressly of the inner connection between the esoteric school at the Goetheanum and the suprasensory Michael School and Michael cultus, and announced that from September he intended going a good deal further with these matters:

> In September, when we…gather again for these Class lessons, it will be the will of the Michael power first to describe the Imaginations of the cultus revelations at the beginning of the nineteenth century. This will be the second stage of lessons. The mantric words that have now penetrated into our souls will come before our soul again in images that—insofar as this is possible—will be pictures, brought down here, of the suprasensory imaginative cultus from the beginning of the nineteenth century.
>
> The third stage of this School will be composed of what can lead us directly toward the interpretations that were given for the mantric words in the suprasensory Michael School of the fifteenth, sixteenth, and seventeenth centuries.[153]

Thus conceived, Steiner was no longer able to give the lessons. But it became apparent that he had wished to enable the Michael community to reexperience and deepen awareness of its own developmental history in the reverse, occult stream of time, so as to be able to fully discover, comprehend, and engage with this. Very probably, Steiner intended giving these lessons in a short span of time, that is, in quick succession, as he had done with the completed nineteen Class lessons of the first stage. Time was pressing, and the esoteric lessons were not an end in themselves. Rather, they were meant as a decisive spiritual aid, helping the community to embark now on the work for twentieth-century civilization that had been in preparation for many centuries—with the support of Michael and in his presence. This presence of Michael was something that could be strongly experienced by participants of the Class lessons of the esoteric school at the Goetheanum. Then, on September 6, 1924, Steiner stated in the first Class Lesson after his return from England:

> My dear friends, you rightly conceive of what is uttered here in this School only if you are aware that what seeks to be introduced into humanity in the presence of the Michael stream itself is spoken here. The words spoken in this School are all Michael words. All resolves of will that are willed in this School are Michael will. You are all pupils of Michael if you properly stand within this School. Only if you bear this awareness within you is it possible to sit in this School in the right way, with the right mood and outlook; to feel yourselves as a member not only of something that enters the world as earthly institution, but of something that does so as heavenly institution.[154]

On another occasion, Steiner went on to say that the content of the Class lessons would only be real if the Michael stream flowed spiritually through the School; he spoke of the tangible presence of Michael in the room where the lessons were held, of his spirit, love, and strength that streamed through the School, blessing its content and enactments. This real presence of the Michael being, the immediate strength of his efficacy, was something that pupils should feel and experience if they were to engage effectively as helpers in the time's challenges and conflicts. *"All these things must live in members' hearts."*[155] On Earth, too, the Michael School was in polar opposition to the Ahriman school. And the might of the Asuras and of Sorath, the Sun demon and opponent of the Christ being in the cosmos, was already active in the 1920s in the hidden background of many conflicts.[156]

Human beings, as Rudolf Steiner wrote in his *Leading Thoughts* in 1924, have the possibility of finding their way out of the sphere of Ahriman to Christ through the image of Michael.[157] By individually realizing this, they also have the capacity to work in community with others—who choose and take the same path—to enable the whole of civilization to find its way from Ahriman's sphere of influence to Christ. The Christ-permeation of civilization, that is, its penetration with living thoughts and powers, its real resurrection, was the task of the School in Dornach. But for this to happen it needed the esoteric Michael School and schooling. If, in union with the workings of the hierarchies, this comes powerfully to effect both in the individual and the community, it has a world-changing potency:

> Michael's impulses are strong, are powerful, and they work from the spiritual realm through the whole human being; they work into the spirit and from there into the soul, and from there into the body of the human being.[158]

In other words, they work also into the substance of the Earth, and thus into all realms of human civilization.

Rudolf Steiner is said to have told Count Polzer-Hoditz on November 11, 1924, that the First Class of the Goetheanum's esoteric School existed for all members of the School for Spiritual Science and that in future, after it had become fully established, it would pass to the responsibility of Ita Wegman.[159] After the Second Class was established, on the other hand, he wished it to be directed by Marie Steiner-von Sivers. This class was intended for thirty-six section leaders and members, lecturers, national leaders and other initiating members. The Third Class would be a kind of master class and have a purely ritual character. He himself would lead this. It would directly address the being of Christ and would be for only twelve future members, identical with the esoteric executive council of the Goetheanum.[160]

Thus strengthened, deepened, and prepared, the Goetheanum and those who would work for it in future, would—as a School for Spiritual Science—engage with and intervene in the conflicts of contemporary civilization. As an active influence within civilization, and a mystery center of the future, the Goetheanum and its School were the center of the General Anthroposophical Society, its inner meaning and real aim. This is very probably why Ludwig Polzer-Hoditz understood the reason for Rudolf Steiner determining Class membership in the way described above. All members of the Dornach School belonged to the First Class. Over and above this, those who took further positions of responsibility within the General Anthroposophical Society and the School should attend the Second Class in order to acquire additional capacities. The latter very likely concerned their social collaboration and that unity of will on which the suprasensory Michael cultus had primarily been focused at the beginning of the nineteenth century.

Finally, as an esoteric *directorate* of the School, Rudolf Steiner conceived an organ composed of twelve people, whose still more advanced schooling would occur in a purely cultic way, and in the spiritual presence of the Christ being. Steiner wanted to have the First and Second Class led by Ita Wegman and Marie Steiner-von Sivers (though subject to his own ultimate responsibility). Instruction in the Third Class, however, should—and must—remain entirely in his hands, also after it had been established.[161]

It was not possible to carry out all this by March 30, 1925, and remained a future undertaking for Steiner. The day before Michaelmas 1924, he rounded off his sublime presentations on the Michael School and the Michael cultus, his esoteric Class lessons—and the whole contents of his teaching in 1924—in a last address that bore the character of a legacy. This brief, twenty-minute address to the members of the Anthroposophical Society ended with the mantric character of the following spiritual testament:[162]

> Spiritual powers springing from
> Sun forces: shining, world-grace bestowing:
> Divine, creative thinking destines you
> To be Michael's dress of rays.
>
> He, the messenger of Christ, endows you
> With holy cosmic will, sustaining us;
> You, the bright beings of ether worlds
> Bear to human beings the Word of Christ.
>
> > So appears the Christ proclaimer
> > To patient, longing, thirsting souls:
> > For them your shining Word streams onward
> > Into the future age of Spirit Man.
> >
> > You, pupils of spirit knowledge
> > Take up Michael's wise direction,
> > Take up the loving Word of cosmic will
> > Actively into your striving souls.[163]

3

Ita Wegman's Path

It is certain that, since Rudolf Steiner's death, the mysteries cannot be further revealed in our time; yet we must continue to cultivate a living, cultic, and not merely intellectual, continuity with the mystery content that he gave, passing this on also to those who did not have the opportunity to know Rudolf Steiner: to those who seek esoteric and not only intellectual connection with him.

LUDWIG POLZER-HODITZ[164]

Auf Geisteshöhen,
An Abgrundesrändern
In uralter Zeiten
Schicksalswende
Gefunden,
Schmiedet Notwendigkeit
Sich nie zu verlieren.
M. lieben Mysa — 13. Januar 1924
Rudolf Steiner

On spiritual heights,
By the edge of the abyss
In primordial times
New destiny
Was found,
Forges the need
Never to lose each other.

To my dear Mysa—January 13 1924
Rudolf Steiner

Rudolf Steiner: A verse written for Ita Wegman

Ita Wegman's interest in Rudolf Steiner's Anthroposophy was esoteric in nature from the very outset.[165] She had encountered Theosophy in the 1990s in Indonesia where she grew up, and in Holland, shortly after Steiner's first appearance in theosophical circles in London in the summer of 1902, she heard about the beginning of spiritual-scientific work under his leadership in Berlin. In the fall of that year she visited him and became one of the first members of his German section of the Theosophical Society, founded in October 1902. Twenty-one years later Steiner referred to this explicitly during the Christmas Foundation Meeting ("She [Ita Wegman] has been a member of our anthroposophic movement for over twenty years. Apart from myself, she has been a member longer than anyone else in the hall."[166])

Although she was living in Berlin, Ita Wegman did not often attend the public lectures that Steiner gave at the Architects' House in that city from 1903 onward because she was looking for direct presentation of modern spiritual science and its suprasensory findings, yet found this largely absent from the programme. ("All German literature and no theosophy, I thought, since the word theosophy did not figure anywhere."[167]) But after a lecture on the spiritual background to Goethe's fairytale of the lily and the green snake, she came closer to him: "After the lecture I asked Steiner whether it would be possible to learn more about esoteric wisdom."[168] As Rudolf Steiner explained in his karma lectures in the summer of 1924, Goethe's fairytale is connected with the Michael cultus at the beginning of the nineteenth century and is an earthly reflection of its cosmic Imaginations:

In the suprasensory world at that time a cultus was established that unfolded in real Imaginations of a spiritual nature. And so one can say that at the end of the eighteenth and beginning of the nineteenth centuries, a suprasensory occurrence hovers in a sphere directly adjoining the physical-sensory world, very close to it—though of course this is meant qualitatively, metaphorically. This is an occurrence embodying suprasensory rites, the elaboration of mighty pictures of spiritual life, of cosmic beings, the beings of the hierarchies, in connection with the great ether influences of the cosmos and with human activities on Earth. It is interesting to find that a particularly favorable moment of this activity of suprasensory rite and cultus, a miniature image of it, if you like, streamed into the mind of Goethe. This miniature image, in altered, metamorphosed form, is what Goethe depicted in his *Fairytale of the Green Snake and the Beautiful Lily.*[169]

It was precisely this content that Ita Wegman was seeking, albeit not fully consciously but out of deep strata of her destiny and will. Following her request Steiner invited her to a session of his esoteric school at the Architects' House, although she was not yet a member of this—only just founded—gathering: "'Come to Motzstrasse 17,' he said to me briefly and significantly and gave me a time and date."[170] Ita Wegman attended the esoteric lesson, which deeply moved her. *"From that moment on, I knew that Rudolf Steiner was my teacher, is my teacher, and will be my teacher in future."*[171]

A few years later, during the Munich Whitsun Congress of the European sections of the Theosophical Society, Rudolf Steiner separated the esoteric school he led from Annie Besant's Esoteric School of Theosophy. At this point his pupils had to decide which path they would pursue in future,[172] and Steiner asked to hear Ita Wegman's decision in person.[173] Rudolf Steiner was already aware at this point who the individuality was before him—as we can see from a retrospective letter he wrote to her on June 11, 1924, from Koberwitz, in which he referred specifically to the Munich congress.[174]

> Soon afterward he asked me to see him. I knew that this would be a decisive moment of my life.... Rudolf Steiner received me with serious demeanor, and a questioning look. Not much was said between us, we understood each other very well. I simply said, since I felt he knew how things stood, *"I will stay with you."* Then his gaze became radiant, he took my hand, gave me the sign of Michael and said important things to me that I may not repeat. A primordial karma existing between him and me was renewed.[175]

Ita Wegman's decision to follow Steiner's path had consequences. In the late fall of 1907, a few months after their meeting in Munich, he began to elaborate the Michael mysteries in his esoteric school. He referred to the members of the school as pupils of Michael and on October 9, 1907, in connection with an account of Christian Rosenkreutz, first spoke of the Michael age that had begun in the fall of 1879.[176]

Ita Wegman later profoundly regretted that these first developments in 1907, in Rudolf Steiner's proximity and in the common mission of destiny within the Michael stream, could not be carried further at that point.[177] The spiritual immediacy of what shone forth in Munich had to recede into the background again: Ita Wegman continued her medical studies in Zurich and lived geographically distant from Rudolf Steiner and the center of the developing Anthroposophical Society. She did not belong to the inner core of people around Steiner, had no direct access to him, and returned to the demands of her personal and professional life—"I only became aware of the scope and importance of this meeting many years later."[178] In a certain respect, Ita Wegman did not stand directly alongside and alone with Rudolf Steiner until the night of the Goetheanum fire, on New Year's Eve 1922/23. In the previous years, of course, she had experienced much within the anthroposophic movement, and also had a hand in shaping it—especially through developing her clinic and anthroposophic pharmaceutics in Arlesheim from early summer 1921. She had also been an eyewitness of the failed battle for social threefolding, and directly involved in the hopeful beginning of the initiative in 1919 in Zurich. Soon afterward she had experienced the enduring tragedy of Central Europe, as well as public dissent surrounding Steiner, and the hatred and scorn toward Anthroposophy, which was defamed and caricatured. In Stuttgart's concert hall, Rudolf Steiner had called out:

> What I represent I do so because the inmost power of my soul insists that I represent it, and because it lives in me in a way that I must stand up for. If it is the truth, then it will make headway despite all opposition...[it] will be realized because truth itself is something spiritual, something divine, and ultimately divine, spiritual truth must be victorious over all powers of enmity.[179]

But he did not have behind him an effective Anthroposophical Society to support him and anthroposophic spiritual science with all its powers, or to fully defend him. Ita Wegman herself was fully preoccupied with her medical endeavors and from 1917, following a suggestion from Steiner, had among other things been pursuing mistletoe and cancer research, and in fact developing this. But increasingly she recognized that an extension of the art of medicine through Anthroposophy was not the only thing necessary in the current times. She also carried in her a longing for the renewal of the mysteries— for medicine and for the whole of culture—which, despite many important lectures and medical courses by Steiner, had still not been satisfied. ("Strong intellectualism in the lectures of the medical courses / my decision to come to Dornach / my surprise at this intellectualism / my longing for a renewal of the mysteries," she wrote briefly and succinctly in one of her notebooks.[180])

Rudolf Steiner had closed his esoteric school at the outbreak of World War I, and did not open it again when it ended. A systematic sequence of esoteric lessons had no longer been taking place for many years,[181] primarily because Steiner did not think that it had been taken up previously in anything like an adequate way. The members' personal need to receive esoteric instructions was as great as ever. But almost no one recognized the connection of such an esoteric schooling—and school—with the spiritual and cultural task of a School for Spiritual Science, in relation also to the protection it offered in the context of contemporary conflicts, and Steiner did not speak about this unasked. One week before the Goetheanum was destroyed by fire, however, in a personal conversation with Ita Wegman and Albert Steffen, he said that he missed in the circles of the Anthroposophical Society a real affirmation of the spirit and the courage to realize spiritual things. Wegman saw his suffering countenance, and *"the impulse awoke deep in my heart to do this."*[182]

In the early morning hours of the night of the fire, Ita Wegman stood alone with Rudolf Steiner at the very edge of the fire, and gazed upon the destruction. Later, after their intense, exoteric and esoteric collaboration began, he looked back to this and other situations of their shared past, which had thrown up numerous tragic situations,[183] and wrote dedicatory words for her in one of his books: "On spiritual heights,

/ By the edge of the abyss / In primordial times / New destiny / Was found, / Forges the need / Never to lose each other."[184]

≈

After the fire, during the course of 1923, Ita Wegman witnessed from the closest proximity Rudolf Steiner's intention to reform the Anthroposophical Society, to awaken it to its intrinsic mission, and indirectly to its karmic background—and the failure of almost all these attempts.[185] Not mincing his words, he spoke of the Anthroposophical Society as "riddled with ahrimanic holes,"[186] and wrote in a private letter: "I am repelled by everything that its executive councils do."[187]

Rudolf Steiner sought in vain to explain to Society functionaries that their community was not some uncommitted experimental field but must take responsibility for the threatened future of civilization, in close connection with already existing anthroposophic endeavors (in education, medicine and social and economic life). But in both the exoteric and esoteric realm, the Anthroposophical Society lagged far behind what he, or rather Anthroposophy itself, needed for its protection and cultivation.

Then, in the summer of 1923, in the ancient mystery landscape of Wales where Steiner was giving wide-ranging lectures, Ita Wegman asked him about the possibility of founding an esoteric school at the Goetheanum, or about the next step necessary in cultivating the new mysteries.[188] Rudolf Steiner answered cautiously, pointing out that esoteric schools cannot be founded on the basis of people's personal will resolves, but are subject to impulses from the world of spirit. But subsequently he evidently approached the world of spirit, or Michael, with Ita Wegman's question or request, and received an affirmative answer. Just as Marie von Sivers's question shortly after the turn of the century had enabled him to initiate an anthroposophic movement within the Theosophical Society,[189] so the *initiative* to establish the esoteric Michael School had issued from Ita Wegman, he said later in a conversation with Count Polzer-Hoditz. (*"The initiative for the esoteric Michael School came, as Rudolf Steiner said, from Frau Dr. Wegman."*[190])

As Emanuel Zeylmans van Emmichoven was able to document in full detail after long and intensive research, Steiner began systematic esoteric instruction or indeed schooling of Ita Wegman immediately after their conversation at Penmaenmawr in Wales.[191] In quick succession she received from Steiner coordinated exercises—mostly in mantric form—which also intensified and spiritually deepened their medical collaboration. After Ita Wegman's death, much evidence was discovered in the correspondence and esoteric material in her literary estate concerning Steiner's close supervision of Wegman's development: *"You walk with me as my friend in worlds of spirit."*[192] In September 1923, shortly after his return from England, their conversations in Penmaenmawr, Wales, and important medical studies in London, he wrote the following verse in her notebook for daily meditation:

> Ever-shining, all-prevailing light:
> To you I entrust my soul.
> May my soul's light weave
> In weaving light of worlds.
> As light I feel myself,
> Light in the small point;
> Light that extends into boundless expanses.
> Light that bears all my being
> Into boundless expanses.
> I feel myself in boundless expanses.

I am pure through-shining light,
I encompass the world of spirits
At the end of my soul of light,
I hold the world of spirits
With my arms of light;
I feel your nearness,
You wish to take me
Into spirit worlds of light.[193]

≈

Rudolf Steiner's spiritual supervision was without doubt of outstanding importance for Ita Wegman. He not only gave her countless exercises but meditated with her—even when he was somewhere else (writing from the agricultural course at Koberwitz, near Breslau, "that I am thinking of you in my meditation and working on your spiritual progress here, too"[194]). But Ita Wegman's presence of mind and resolve to act, her continually developing awareness of the historical situation and his mission within it, was also of very major significance for Rudolf Steiner: "This process of two people who work alongside each other, each necessary to the other..."[195]

Ludwig Polzer-Hoditz, very probably the only one to hold discussions with Steiner after he fell ill about the First Class, later referred to Ita Wegman as his (Steiner's) "helper in founding and developing the mysteries," and spoke of the "esoteric union of destiny" as a "condition for the mysteries in the modern age."[196] "*Support shall be for me / Your understanding / Your love and faithfulness. / I see grow up / Out of your understanding / The light that shines to me. / I see grow up / Out of your love / The warmth that blesses me. / I see grow up / Out of your faithfulness / The air that enlivens me,*" wrote Steiner to and for Wegman.[197]

The available documents offer no insights into how Wegman experienced the beginning of the esoteric Class lessons in the joinery workshop on February 15, 1924, and whether Steiner had previously spoken to her about the sequence of the lessons and the aim of the whole undertaking. However, she pursued the path to the true "I" indicated in the Class lessons, out of the darkness of earthly "I"-consciousness and humanity's spiritual situation since the nineteenth century; and there is much to suggest that she recognized clearly from the outset how important this modern path of schooling and development was for the individual and the community. Ita Wegman never revealed, verbally or in writing, when Steiner had first spoken to her in detail about the suprasensory School of Michael, and what exactly he said to her. All that she stated was this: *"I heard many things about this School from Rudolf Steiner, also regarding my and his connection with it."*[198]

Soon after the First Class started, Wegman also realized what future relevance it could have for building the spiritual community around the Goetheanum and its School for Spiritual Science. Six months previously, she had asked Steiner to establish an esoteric school and initiate a new mystery center in Dornach, and this was because she had seen from the struggles of the previous year that shared anthroposophic endeavor not only needed a new form but a new spiritual impetus so as to develop into the future and to meet this future in the right way. She was concerned first and foremost with establishing a bedrock for Anthroposophy, as Steiner stated in 1924 in relation to the Class community, and with representing the "anthroposophic cause to the world": *"Specifically through this school the seriousness that is absolutely necessary for the anthroposophic movement to properly, spiritually thrive will be able to shine into it."*[199]

With Ita Wegman, whom Steiner described on August 28, 1924, in London as "his friend and colleague in the medical domain and in other fields of spiritual research,"[200] Steiner was able subsequently to develop the field of medicine within the School in a very dynamic way. He was able not only to undertake organological research with her—as he described in the summer of 1924 in two singular presentations in Torquay, England, expressly connecting this research with the shared enquiries of teacher and pupil at Ephesus[201]—but also initiated teaching and training with her in the School's medical department. Assisted by her, immediately after the Christmas Foundation Meeting ended, Steiner began his mantrically structured schooling course for the young doctors (on January 2, 1924), which de facto became the first course of the School. Three months later he admitted the whole group of young doctors into the School, establishing with Ita Wegman the organ of newsletters for the group, of which he also spoke in the Class lessons, thus modeling the first esoteric community within a School section.[202] He spoke to the young doctors about their "connection with us here,"[203] and at the end of the first course, on January 9, 1924, took his farewell from them with these words:

> Let us remain united with one another in this sense, my dear friends; let us remain united so that you retain your focus and center here at the Goetheanum in Dornach, and really hold to this center, *so that it can work through you in the world.*[204]

What Rudolf Steiner was able to model in this way with Ita Wegman in the field of medicine, as an esoteric and exoteric practice of research, teaching, training, and application,[205] giving tangible visibility to the character of the School, was exemplary for the whole further development in Dornach: for what "is really intended by the Goetheanum today in relation to the development of the world and civilization."[206]

Parallel to all these developments—the series of esoteric Class lessons, the ongoing schooling of Ita Wegman (which without doubt was *also* a preparation for the tasks that she was to take on), their common clinical and research work, the medical courses Steiner gave, and all his other work to realize the Christmas Foundation Meeting and develop the School for Spiritual Science with its various sections[207]—the karma lessons continued, and with them the elaboration of the Michael theme. In a review in one of her notebooks, composed for a lecture, Ita Wegman wrote as follows of the summer of 1924 and Rudolf Steiner:

> He told me [at that time] that people should now know that the Class was the Michael School in the world of spirit. He was the leader of this school, and I his helper and colleague. It was my task to protect the mantras: people must turn to me or to him if a member wished to give another the mantras. This was an esoteric act, the beginning of a newly beginning esotericism. At the same time, admission was arranged so that the prospective member would hear these words: *"This is the Michael School, which is led by myself and Frau Wegman."*[208]

In another recollection Wegman also recorded the mode of admission to the School and its First Class—or the Michael School of the spiritual world—as introduced in September 1924:

> From now on admissions took place in the studio. I had to stand next to the Doctor, and Dr. Wachsmuth led

members in. Dr. Steiner asked the prospective member a few questions, and if he was admitted, Dr. Steiner spoke the following words: "If you wish to remain faithful to the Michael School, give me your hand. Give your hand also to Frau Dr. Wegman, who will direct the Michael School with me.[209]

Until this time, admissions to the First Class had been accomplished largely without such formality: following written request to Steiner, the latter had approved (or in some cases refused) admission.[210] Now however, as Wegman reported, Rudolf Steiner introduced a brief but clear admission ritual, and obliged her to take part in this. In a letter that referred to this retrospectively, one of the newly admitted Class members wrote, "On September 5, 1924, Rudolf Steiner admitted me to the First Class. After a handshake and an associated pledge of faithfulness, he also had me give my hand to the co-leader of the Class, Frau Dr. Wegman who was sitting beside him."[211] In all Class lessons given in Dornach from September 6, 1924, onward, Steiner emphasized Ita Wegman's special joint responsibility for the mantras of these cultic lessons and for the esoteric school as such.[212]

≈

The September sessions of the First Class were by no means merely repeat lessons in the conventional sense, but brought new qualities to light. Despite the new energy and impetus that Rudolf Steiner displayed after the Christmas Foundation Meeting, the previous months of 1924 had certainly not been easy. Although Steiner had done all in his power to fully realize the impulse of the Christmas Foundation Meeting and to establish the School quickly, Society members, including many who held positions of responsibility within it, lagged far behind what had actually been accomplished and the seeds that had been planted, in the joinery workshop at the turn of the year. In 1931, in a lecture in London, Ita Wegman said:

> It seemed that this [event of the Christmas Foundation Meeting] had been taken up with great enthusiasm. But did people really admit it into their hearts? The call of the elemental spirits, invoked as witnesses in the laying of the foundation stone, the plea "...may human beings hear it," did not achieve what they should have done; human ears remained deaf, and the elemental spirits, hopefully expectant of what might come from humankind, grew restless when insufficient response came from human beings. This is what Dr. Steiner told me. And he spoke of a promise that he had made to the world of spirit, and that he must keep if things did not change.[213]

Rudolf Steiner spoke of these problems already in the second lesson, and this theme ran through the rest of the lessons too in the form of introductory words and concluding comments. It even sealed the spiritual culmination of the lessons at the end of the nineteenth.[214] The First Class was intended not only to establish a bedrock for Anthroposophy but its members should at least do what Steiner still found painfully lacking among many in the Anthroposophical Society, including those in positions of responsibility: understand the Christmas Foundation Meeting and draw the necessary consequences—of taking it and the whole of Anthroposophy seriously, and committing themselves fully to working for it. Back in May 1924, Steiner had said in Paris, "A discrepancy exists, I have to say, between what I will and intend, what is said to members out of this will, and what members take up and understand."[215] Of a meeting with Steiner around this same time, Friedrich Rittelmeyer wrote that he "seemed almost crushed by the failure of his adherents."[216] "Among anthroposophists," said Steiner, "there is far too little serious regard for what actually is flowing through the anthroposophic movement..."[217]

Steiner continued nevertheless. In the summer, on successive occasions, he elaborated further on the connections between the suprasensory Michael School and the spiritual history, the karma of the Anthroposophical Society. In London at the end of August, for the first time he concluded a Class ritually, using the seal and sign of Michael ("In the sign of Michael we receive what thus approaches us..."[218]) and emphasizing Ita Wegman's shared responsibility for the mantras:

> The verses and content of the lessons can only be communicated to members of the esoteric school, thus to those who hold a blue card. Those unable to be present can receive the verses from others who were here. But in every single instance, someone who wishes to pass on the verses must ask permission for this from Dr. Wegman or myself. It is part of the esoteric leadership of these lessons that the factual reality of a request must reach us in every instance.[219]

In September, Steiner once again emphatically accentuated the Michael dimension, power, and significance of the esoteric lessons, and indeed of the esoteric school of the Goetheanum, as if he wished to give its members one last chance to fully recognize the reality of these contexts and their connection with his accounts in the karma lectures, so that they might finally achieve an existential breakthrough and find the commitment to protect this spiritual initiative. He began the first lesson in September, in Dornach, with a striking reflection on the "impulse of the Christmas

Foundation Meeting and the laying of the spiritual foundation stone of the Anthroposophical Society" and the core of its esoteric activity in the esoteric school of the Goetheanum. He then passed on to a detailed account of the time spirit Michael in relation to humanity's evolutionary periods, each subject to the sway of an archangel, since Golgotha: "And so, my dear friends, let us be aware that the Michael impulses live as I have described in all that should exist in our time as spiritual activity and spiritual being."[220] Then, with unmistakable clarity, Steiner emphasized the First Class's relation to Michael, and the fact that it belonged to the Michael stream, a theme he had been speaking of very intently in karma lectures of the previous weeks, formulating sentences we quoted earlier:

> And only then, my dear friends, do you rightly conceive of what is uttered here in this School if you are aware that only what seeks to be introduced into humanity in the presence of the Michael stream itself is spoken here. The words spoken in this School are all Michael words. All resolves of will that are willed in this School are Michael will. You are all pupils of Michael if you properly stand within this School. Only if you bear this awareness within you is it possible to sit in this School in the right way, with the right mood and outlook; to feel yourselves as a member not only of something that enters the world as earthly institution, but of something that does so as heavenly institution.[221]

The Archai Michael, he said, had not only founded the esoteric school of the Goetheanum, but also inspires and leads it. Likewise the Guardian of the Threshold, of such outstanding importance during the course of esoteric schooling, was a serving part of the Michael power and his first representative and viceroy at the threshold to the land of spirit.[222]

≈

In the days preceding the Class lesson of September 6, Rudolf Steiner had performed a cultic ritual with Ita Wegman, at the end of which she received his rose cross: "...I received his cross...directly from him: he removed it from around his neck and gave it to me, saying, '*From this moment onward we are both present together for the Michael School.*'"[223] The text of the ritual or cultic service (Wegman) that Steiner wrote down for Wegman in the form of a recollection meditation, was only identified among her posthumous papers, and contextualized, in 2010[224]). In this transcript the whole process of ritual encounter with the spirit leader also culminates in the handing over of the rose cross ("...then Michael leads us into the true Rosicrucian School" as was first written at the cultic end of the lesson of September 6, 1924[225]).

The connection with the being who, in his incarnation as John, was initiated by Jesus Christ, and later wrote the Gospel of John and the Apocalypse, was of major importance for accomplishment of the First Class, which shows how light begins to shine forth from the darkness—out of the awakened, true human "I."[226] The two mantras of primary importance in the first part of the ritual process of admitting Ita Wegman into her (joint) responsibility for the First Class, revealed qualities connected with the beings of Christian Rosenkreutz and Master Jesus, who accompanied Rudolf Steiner and his mission in the nineteenth and twentieth centuries;[227] they came to be of decisive importance for Ita Wegman's further path and her whole stance and outlook in the difficult forthcoming years:

Primal powers sustain me
Spirits of fire free me
Spirits of light illumine me
So that I reach toward spirit being
So that I feel the beings of soul
So that I walk safe over uncertainties
So that I stand above abysses

....

In me live the Christ
And transform my breath
And warm the flow of my blood
And shine before my being of soul.[228]

"From this moment onward we are both present together for the Michael School," said Rudolf Steiner after accomplishing the cultic rite and giving his rose cross to Ita Wegman. Doubtless this occurrence underlay the new admission rite for Class members from September 1924 onward. ("Give your hand also to Frau Dr. Wegman, who will lead the Michael School with me"); and it was intrinsic to the final intensification of the Michael impulse that Steiner wished to and had to undertake while still alive.

As early as 1907, no doubt, when Steiner heard Wegman's decision to adhere to his esoteric school, and when he took her hand and gave her the Michael sign, he knew how closely connected Wegman's eternal individuality was with the Michael stream and Michael himself. It was not accidental that, in the summer of 1923, Wegman asked Steiner to establish the Michael School as foundation for the new, Christian mysteries, even if she did not, as yet, have a clear vision of its whole context and scope. Yet her higher "I" worked in will deeds such as this, and Rudolf Steiner knew who he had before him. *"Mysa stands under Mikael / transfigured,"* he had written on

June 26, 1924, shortly after the festival of St. John the Baptist, [229] using the name given her in the mysteries of Ephesus. A few days later, on July 1, in the joinery workshop, he had begun to illumine the destinies of the Dominican community in his karma lectures, thus embarking on his accounts of the Michael community.

≈

When Rudolf Steiner fell ill at the end of September 1924, Ita Wegman was at his side uninterruptedly. He told her that the members' dead thoughts and the lack of understanding were what had paralyzed[230] him. She had to stand by and witness what the deaf ears of members and the promise he had given the world of spirit, actually meant for him.[231] In her draft for her London lecture of February 27, 1931, she wrote:

> I will pass over the painful hours, weeks, and months when I attended his sickbed in the joinery workshop studio. It actually isn't possible to describe the battles fought in these silent watches against the onslaught of hostile powers. (And if I also offer the image that occurred so often to me, that of Catholic priests who wished evil on him, you can understand how much suffering he underwent in his illness.)[232]

In a notebook at the time when Steiner was ill, she wrote down something Rudolf Steiner said: *"Every night the battles recur, they can render themselves invisible, which is why they are so dangerous. They cause a very great deal of harm. Klingsor unfolds his whole power <u>against</u> me."*[233]

Already in the months after the Christmas Foundation Meeting, Ita Wegman realized how fraught with conflict was the impulse of the new mysteries, and the existential risk Steiner had taken upon himself with his deed.[234] He repeatedly spoke to her about the actions of the anti-Michael demons, Klingsor also among them ("Many of these threats / I have known, / have partly understood / have partly not understood. / To understand everything fully / would be so terrible / that it remains concealed from me / (Inner paralyses could follow) / But I must continue" [Notebook, April 1925][235]). Rudolf Steiner had told her that the anthroposophic community needed to achieve a breakthrough for and with Michael's activity by Michaelmas 1924, or else he would fall sick. Knowing this, he had intensified his lecturing activities and the Class lessons from July onward. For Wegman's schooling he had also given her various mantras that spoke directly of the actions of the (anti-Michael) demons, which must be opposed with the aid of Michael:

> *...So that light might grow,*
> *Where, without this deed,*
> *Eternal darkness would hold sway.*
> *Such a place exists:*
> *It must vanish;*
> *Make it one day vanish.*
> *So speaks, admonishing,*
> *Michael's gaze.*[236]

Subsequently, Ita Wegman did all in her power to support Rudolf Steiner in this spiritual battle. She knew that he was relying on her, and he gave clear expression to this in his further esoteric transcripts, in which, however, it was not he himself speaking but the spirit powers accompanying his work, including Michael first and foremost:

> Complement him with your understanding
> As he fulfillls his spiritual task

Of which an image is embodied
In his earthly work's accomplishment.
We need his spirit path's expanse,
He needs your being's fellowship.[237]

But Ita Wegman had understood at an early stage that she
alone would not be able to sufficiently protect Rudolf Steiner.
This was no doubt also connected with his recurring appeal to
people to awaken, to take the Christmas Foundation Meeting
seriously and realize it, or in other words fulfill the destined
mission of the Michael community on Earth as he had especially formulated this to Class members. In order to work further on Earth and successfully wage the battle with the anti-
Michael demons, Rudolf Steiner needed the uncompromising
support of the Anthroposophical Society and its esoteric core,
which he saw as the community of School members. But real
knowledge of the situation and the task at hand offered no
hope of the required protection and the consciousness necessary for providing it, despite the whole Christmas Foundation event in 1924. Ita Wegman did whatever she could, also
in her medical treatment of Steiner: he gave her and Ludwig
Noll suggestions for the treatment he desired, including actual
medicines.[238] Despite her capacities and her courage to heal,
as well as Rudolf Steiner's enormous gratitude for her untiring
devotion,[239] in retrospect she did not think that her capacities
had been sufficient for the task of saving Rudolf Steiner. But
she did not by any means see this lack as connected with the
medical field, saying just six years after his death in London:

...Here I have to interject that I myself suffer unspeakably when I reflect that I may not have done everything
possible to understand the Christmas Foundation Meeting.
And the responsibility that weighs on me for failing to be

as wakeful as I would have wished during Rudolf Steiner's last year, despite being in his proximity daily for hours at a time, is unspeakably hard to bear.[240]

Unlike almost all other Society and School members, Ita Wegman had been very much awake through the experiences of 1924. Nevertheless, her consciousness was not at the level of Steiner's nor of what would really have been needed. She knew that a far greater spiritual strength would have been necessary to effectively protect Rudolf Steiner, and to heal his body.

The day after Steiner died, in despair and tears, she had spoken of this with her executive council colleague Albert Steffen. However he took her words as an expression of her personal failure, recording them in his diary for posterity three days later in his own fashion and with his own interpretation.[241] Albert Steffen's awareness of the deed of the Christmas Foundation Meeting, of the existential danger that Steiner had entered into by this deed, and his whole situation in 1924, bore no comparison to Ita Wegman's consciousness of this.[242] He had no inkling of most of the circumstances involved, had failed to understand the specific karmic context of Steiner's evening lectures during the Christmas Foundation Meeting, nor did he know of Ita Wegman's participation in and joint responsibility for the First Class or of her esoteric schooling by Rudolf Steiner since the summer of 1923. Her words to him after Steiner's death had not been some kind of confession,[243] but an honest and despairing outcry from a leading spiritual pupil of Steiner's who knew that the anthroposophic community—along with every single member in it, including herself—had failed to give Steiner the protection he needed and thus bore heavy guilt. ("*...this death, for which* *we are all no doubt together to blame, both as individuals and as Society...*" Marie Steiner-von Sivers, 1942[244]) But Albert Steffen interpreted her words as indicative of her own, private esoteric failure, and he repeatedly returned to this view in crisis meetings of the executive council. In a meeting on November 29, 1930, Ita Wegman defended herself against this repeated accusation, and spoke of an affront to her honor, at which Albert Steffen said: "No, Frau Dr. Wegman, your honor is not in question, but you failed as an esotericist. This is not an affront to the honor of any person, but just to say that you failed to reach a certain level..."[245]

≈

In the—somewhat threadbare—program for the Easter festival of the General Anthroposophical Society shortly after Steiner's death, Ita Wegman found there was no Class lesson.[246] Despite being a member of the esoteric executive council she had not been involved in any way in shaping the program.[247] Thereupon she requested that the esoteric lessons should be included in the forthcoming large conferences. She knew from Steiner, and her accompaniment of him throughout 1924, how important he considered it for the future to develop, through the First Class, an esoteric core in the Anthroposophical Society. ("She regarded the Class lessons as the core element of all conferences." Emanuel Zeylmans van Emmichoven[248]) Despite Steiner's death, Wegman felt that she retained shared responsibility for realizing the Christmas Foundation Meeting; and from her own outlook and vision it was clear to her how necessary it would be to realize spiritual-social impulses in the contested fields of contemporary culture. In medicine, curative education, and the life of society she felt she must continue to work for the

Michael stream and against the anti-Michael demons, needing for this the intensification of Anthroposophy that had been made possible by the Christmas Foundation Meeting and the refounding of the School. In his concluding lecture at the Christmas Foundation Meeting, Steiner had hinted at the extraordinary quantity of destructive substance present in the contemporary world: "Powers are at work that give us an intimation of the kinds of abyss into which Western civilization is still to plunge."

By now these developments had long been apparent in the advance of civilization. Ita Wegman had understood—and Steiner had also personally enlightened her on this—how much would depend in this situation on whether the Michael stream succeeded in introducing the content of the karma lectures and the Class lessons into the common will of members so that, thus strengthened and united, they could incorporate the fruits of Anthroposophy into civilization.[249] She bore joint responsibility—though this was fiercely contested by all her executive council colleagues apart from Elisabeth Vreede—for the First Class, which Rudolf Steiner said would be *the only way* in which the anthroposophic movement would sustain its real spiritual strength. In the conflicts within this council that had existed already in Rudolf Steiner's lifetime,[250] and dramatically intensified after March 30, 1925,[251] she was however accorded the role of secretary in relation to the Class.[252]

In fact, Albert Steffen was by no means the only one among the leading functionaries who had almost entirely failed to notice what transpired between Rudolf Steiner and Ita Wegman since the summer of 1923, even though this belonged intrinsically and intimately to the substance of the whole Christmas Foundation Meeting.[253]

In the second month after Rudolf Steiner's death, after fruitless discussions within the executive council, Ita Wegman decided to hold a Class lesson in Paris (May 25, 1925, during the annual general meeting of the French national society) and informed her colleagues of this in advance. Subsequently she continued to do this, with a Michaelic, cosmopolitan orientation, in Prague, Vienna, and London, as well as in Stuttgart, Cologne and Hamburg.[254] She was aware that Steiner himself had intended and also instigated this expansion. ("At the time it was the intention of our teacher, to personally establish Class lessons, to begin with, in various other centers of Germany and [other] national societies."[255] Ita Wegman was concerned *"through repetition to bring to living effect in the members the powers that lie in this esotericism."*[256] She was thinking particularly of members whose place of residence and life situation had largely prevented them from attending more than (at best) one or two introductory Class lessons given by Rudolf Steiner, and therefore were entirely ignorant of the organism of the nineteen lessons of the course[257] even though they belonged to the General Anthroposophical Society and the Michael community.

In the prewar year of 1913/14, Steiner had said that the content of the Fifth Gospel would be *urgently needed* in humanity's evolution in the very near future: "The souls that now absorb it will very certainly need it for the soul-spiritual work they must accomplish in the further course of humanity's evolution."[258] Precisely the same was true, although to a far greater degree, of the content of the Class lessons, which also had a special connection with the Fifth Gospel.[259] What Steiner had intended and initiated with the Christmas

Foundation Meeting had to be continued, and in Ita Wegman's view it was not possible to do this exclusively in Dornach, thus excluding countless people from the content and path of the available Class lessons. Ita Wegman wished to pass on unaltered to members the Michael words that Rudolf Steiner had spoken; and while he was still alive, and with his support, she had received the transcripts of the lessons from Helene Finckh. ("He entrusted me with the task of concerning myself intensively with the Michael School; and when I said that I did not yet have the shorthand transcripts, he allowed me to request these from Frau Finckh, also signing the letter that I wrote to her as the official shorthand typist."[260])

It was with great humility that Wegman held the class in Paris, and subsequent lessons in Prague, Vienna, London, and elsewhere.

> ...She read in a calm, and entirely objective manner, in the rhythm of Rudolf Steiner's speech, in which she was fully immersed. She read fluently, selflessly and in a medium pitch; naturally and simply, with great presence of mind, and in the atmosphere of an esoteric lesson characterized by humility and reticence; she was enveloped in this aura.[261]

She never referred to her key collaboration with Steiner in the Michael movement, her importance in facilitating the First Class and the Christmas Foundation Meeting, let alone her karmic connection with Steiner. Her demeanor was one of objectivity, reticence, and presence of mind.[262] She tried, despite enormously difficult circumstances, to uphold the responsibility she had accepted, and in particular to keep faith with events in September 1924, including the ritual for admitting new School members. In a report for the newsletter about the events in Paris in May 1925, and the first Class lesson given there since Steiner's death, she wrote:

> When Dr. Steiner founded this First Class of the School for Spiritual Science, he appointed me as his colleague. At that time, newly admitted pupils, those who had not formerly studied esotericism, promised to be faithful members of the School. This is why, after the death of our teacher Dr. Steiner, I do not feel I have relinquished these duties. On the contrary, I feel more beholden to them than ever, for what Rudolf Steiner instituted I must regard as realities of the spiritual world. And so the task fell to me to engage in a repetition of the esoteric lessons of the School for Spiritual Science given by Dr. Steiner. And, to my great satisfaction, the first step in doing so has been taken in Paris.[263]

A quite different quality of inwardness held sway during the lessons themselves or in her introductory words to them, which Wegman developed in the esoteric context of the classes: "And so, my dear friends, I wish to stand here before you and give you again the words of Rudolf Steiner, to continue his love and his faithfulness to you, in as far as this lies in my powers."[264]

≈

Ita Wegman held the lessons in the unaltered wording of Steiner's, having experienced all that lay in these words between February 15 and September 20, 1924. The content of the Class lessons was a part of Rudolf Steiner's spiritual biography, that is, of his objective experiences in communication with the world of spirit, its beings and processes: an acquiring of the Christ consciousness of the true "I."[265] Rudolf Steiner had taken responsibility for every word of the lessons before the angelic powers over-lighting the anthroposophic movement;

and he had described the whole School as a body of something "that flows out of the life of spirit itself."[266] ("And thus in everything that occurs in such a School is manifest the outer expression of a reality and activity that really takes place in the suprasensory, spiritual world itself."[267]) The repetition of the lessons implied for Ita Wegman the need to take up or instigate an esoteric relationship with Rudolf Steiner, and thus—however objective and transpersonal their tone, sequence, and overall composition—to maintain the connection of the lessons with Rudolf Steiner's spiritual individuality. Both during his lifetime and afterward Rudolf Steiner had wished to guide the medical Section *through* the lessons.[268]

A year after the Goetheanum was destroyed by fire—an event which also placed great strain on his own constitution[269]—he had initiated the Christmas Foundation Meeting and the new founding of the School in a state that was already greatly compromised. He knew that he would not survive for further decades to oversee the development and elaboration of the School on Earth. But he had spoken for almost two decades and in many details about the after-death activity of the dead, and Ita Wegman was aware that the organ of the esoteric executive council *also* was and should become an instrument for the continuing strength of inspiration and intuition of his being and the powers connected with it after he had crossed the threshold.

Steiner had repeatedly and insistently described how Christian Rosenkreutz actively stood by the members of his community even in an excarnated condition, and exerted a spiritual influence;[270] and to Wegman he had personally entrusted numerous mantras that spoke of such a form of collaboration. With this in view, she felt obliged to carry into the future the stream of Class lessons developed between February and September 1924, without having any means, or even the aspiration, to go beyond what Rudolf Steiner had given. In addition she felt obliged to acquaint members with the central contents of the karma courses in so far as they related to the Michael background to the Anthroposophical Society, that is, its destiny and its mission. Ita Wegman had witnessed Rudolf Steiner's desire, during his illness, to look through Frau Finckh's transcripts of the karma lectures and prepare them for publication, because assimilation and realization of their contents was of such decisive importance for the future.

After his death, however, nothing of this kind was published for many—decisive—years. Marie Steiner-von Sivers did not publish the first volume of the karma lectures until 1933, more than eight years after the Christmas Foundation Meeting, at a time when central Europe's terrible destiny had already been sealed. For Ita Wegman all this was incomprehensible, and, in view of the world situation and that of the Michael community, also irresponsible, although she kept quiet about it. Steiner had been most urgent and emphatic in insisting that, given the approaching influx of dark powers into politics and society, everything would depend in the near future on making the School and its civilizing influence true and effective, and that this would depend on the united forces of the Michaelites' esoteric karmic community, on their wakeful awareness as they lived and worked in contexts he had described in the karma lectures. In this situation Ita Wegman did the little she was still able to, attempting in essays she wrote for the internal newsletter to continue the core intention of the *Leading Thoughts* (which focused on the theme of Christ–Michael), and to publicize to Society members the key contents of Rudolf Steiner's lectures in 1924.[271] She also held the Class lessons wherever this was possible. Inwardly, in an ever more tense and in fact toxic anthroposophic atmosphere, amid a developing global tragedy and its destructive materials, she remained authentic, healthy, and active for many years with the mantric substance given her by Rudolf Steiner. Likewise the words that had been part of the ritual of her acceptance into shared responsibility for the First Class proved their enduring and in fact increasing relevance—*"So that I walk safe over uncertainties / So that I stand above abysses..."*

It was and remained Ita Wegman's great concern to unfold the full dignity and strength of the esoteric lessons. As Rudolf Steiner had said, Michael blesses and strengthens the lessons through his presence, with his spirit. In September 1924 Steiner had spoken of the lessons as occult services through which the Michael pupils would receive the mantras.[272] The esoteric lessons culminated in these mantras; and yet the non-mantric content and formulations of the lessons were also Michael words ("Michael words are *all* the words that are spoken in this School."[273]) As Ita Wegman saw it, the lessons' esoteric dimension and efficacy, and thus the power of the presence of Michael, were of central importance for the continuation of the anthroposophic movement on Earth. Thus she wished to hold the lessons in this spiritual awareness, with warmth, inwardness, and reverence. They were not a substitute for conventional worship, and Steiner did not hold the Class lessons on Sunday but wherever possible on a Friday evening. At the same time he emphasized at the Christmas Foundation Meeting that in future it would be a matter of regarding the anthroposophic movement "in its entirety, with all its detailed aspects [as] a worship and service to the gods, rather than mistaking it for a purely earthly service":

> And we find the right mood for the movement if we see it in its entirety as divine worship, divine service of this kind. And as such let us take it into our hearts at the beginning of this conference of ours; let us inscribe deeply in our hearts how this anthroposophic movement seeks to unite the soul of every single individual who dedicates himself to it with the originating sources of everything human in the world of spirit, how this anthroposophic movement seeks to lead the human being to the latest, provisional form of enlightenment in humanity's evolution on Earth, one that can for the time being satisfy us and that, as developing revelation, we can can clothe in these words: *Yes, this is what I am as human being, as God-willed human being on Earth, as God-willed human being in the universe.*[274]

This was also the precise goal of esoteric instruction, participation in which could enable School members to learn to experience themselves as essentially connected with the Word of worlds, the Logos—as "God-willed human being in the universe," as an "I" willed by the world of spirit. Were it to prove possible in future for the Michaelites to experience and recognize themselves in this dimension of their self—both individually and in community—then they would be able to set to work to fulfill the mission for civilization that was assigned them by destiny, and was connected with the Christ-permeation of the Earth. Earthly "I"-consciousness needed to develop gradually toward Christ consciousness if it were really to be equal to the challenge of this Christ-permeation of diverse fields of life and practice in the contemporary context, given present threats and aims.[275] Esoteric schooling sought to enable the true "I" to begin to shine in pupils of Michael; they could and should become the light of the world, and bear this light—as that of the true, authentic human being—into the darkness. "For with this light we can help to redeem our fellow human beings and all kingdoms of nature" (Sergei O. Prokofieff).[276] Many years before the Christmas Foundation Meeting, the refounding of the School for Spiritual Science and the inauguration of its medical, pedagogical, scientific, artistic, and religious sections, Rudolf Steiner had already written in his book, *How to Know Higher Worlds*: "*We should partake of the spirit so that we can bear its revelations into the world of the senses. Human beings transform the Earth by implanting in it what they discovers from spirit land; therein lies their mission.*"[277]

The esoteric School at the Goetheanum had been established by the powers "that live close to the Earth and bring about the healing of humanity,"[278] and were observing the contemporary situation with the greatest concern. The second Mystery of Golgotha in the etheric realm, and the processes leading to it, that is, the spread of the black cloud of materialism in the world of spirit, were by no means yet concluded, despite the fifth sacrificial deed of Christ and the Nathan soul.[279] The distortion and successive deformation and darkening of the image of the human being that had only begun in the nineteenth century, continued unabated. It was now in the process of causing practical consequences on Earth, with resulting effects in the world of spirit. For years, with the deepest concern, Ita Wegman had been carefully observing the whole course of contemporary, social-Darwinian and economically motivated debates on euthanasia, with its aim, influenced by the anti-Michael demons, of "destroying lives not worth living."[280]

On February 12, 1933, one of Wegman's leading colleagues, Werner Pache, wrote in a letter to her:

> We would like to ask you once again to try to arrange to
> pass through Hamborn on your way back from England
> and give a Class lesson here. The day before yesterday I
> was standing at Wittenbergplatz in Berlin where, as in
> many other public squares, loudspeakers were blasting out
> speeches by Hitler, and the power of Ahriman was almost
> overwhelming. Suddenly, I felt a very reassuring sense of
> tranquility—it was so strong that it released me instantly
> from the thrall of this evil might. It was a sense that our
> cause will not founder.[281]

In his first speech as German Chancellor, Adolf Hitler,
introduced by Joseph Goebbels, outlined his future policies in
Berlin's Palace of Sport on February 10, 1933. Werner Pache
experienced here the almost overwhelming power of Ahriman, and immediately turned to Wegman to ask her to visit
the curative home at Schloss Hamborn (near Paderborn) once
again, and give an esoteric Class lesson for leading colleagues
who were all members of the School. Pache felt the need to
intensify the community's Michaelic strength. *"Then I will be
among you..."* Steiner had told Anna Samweber on November 10, 1923, the day after Adolf Hitler's first attempt at a
putsch in Munich, as he gave her the mantra, "To Friends
in Berlin" to strengthen them in forthcoming times of great
difficulty.[282] To hold a Class lesson in the wording given by
Steiner was, in this situation, anything other than a "backward-looking means of relying on sacred tradition in the form
of preserved texts,"[283] nor a "backward-looking, preservation-
ist stance,"[284] but rather an indispensable element of spiritual
community-building and spiritual resistance, and a unique
source of strength, courage, and spiritual assurance, as Werne

Pache knew from experience. Working with children in need of special care, he and his colleagues were in an exposed position, and he was resolved not to allow his cause to go under. Nine years before Werner Pache's letter to Wegman, on April 11, 1924, Rudolf Steiner had said the following in his seventh Class lesson:[285]

> We will have a very hard time with Anthroposophy, and the members of the School must know that they must help endure these difficulties. They are, after all, not just anthroposophists, but also members of an esoteric School.

≈

Ita Wegman, keeping fully abreast of contemporary developments and, during 1933, making tireless efforts to build up Michaelic centers for Anthroposophy in England, and create emigration networks for those threatened by the Hitler regime,[286] gave her utmost support to Werner Pache and the Hamborn community. And yet she received no support or backing from the Goetheanum. On the contrary, she was increasingly marginalized and eventually completely excluded in 1934/35—that is, dismissed from all her offices and duties.[287] Thus the fundamental concept of the School for Spiritual Science, as Steiner had developed this with Wegman's decisive help, was largely in ruins at a critical historical time—*"that the School for Spiritual Science with its diverse sections must form a core for everything that should in turn work esoterically within the Anthroposophical Society...."*[288]

After a severe illness that brought her close to death in the spring of 1934—and gave her a profound spiritual experience—Ita Wegman withdrew entirely from all further Goetheanum-related conflicts.[289] She told her friends in

Arlesheim and in many other countries, in personal conversations and letters, that henceforth she would focus entirely on her work in medicine, curative education, and the esoteric School with the Class lessons. She would, she said, return to Rudolf Steiner's founding esoteric impulse with the Michael School and the Christmas Foundation Meeting, and place this at the center of her work without any reference to the Society leaders in Dornach and the situation there.[290]

After the deeply incisive caesura of 1934 and '35, Ita Wegman began through her Class work to gather around her people for whom a connection to Michael and the esoteric dimension of the Christmas Foundation Meeting was central—not groups of people but individuals who were prepared to pursue spiritual development above and beyond all Society conflicts and schisms, and *thereby* to achieve a rediscovery and intensification of their Michaelic community. ("Individuals count now, and, through the development of each they must create a higher association together whose roots are in the world of spirit. This preserves the individualized development and freedom of every person. Through insight as individuals, each person feels connected with this spirit union or Michael School."[291]) She told them that Rudolf Steiner's originating impulse of the Christmas Foundation Meeting had sought to form the Anthroposophical Society into a vessel into which the esoteric wisdom of Michael and his School could flow.

In 1934 and '35, Wegman had been forced to recognize that it was no longer possible to create this vessel at the Goetheanum under the given circumstances, and in the national societies dependent on it. But she very much endeavored to work spiritually to ensure that in future this vessel—even if only after a long period—could arise again in purity ("it may be

that this can only happen in human hearts"[292]). She doubtless regarded the lessons of the First Class, for which she still,
as ever, retained spiritual-esoteric responsibility, as a central
aspect of this work for the future. If it should one day prove
possible to enable the General Anthroposophical Society, the
School for Spiritual Science and its First Class to emerge again
in the form intended by Rudolf Steiner, then this must issue
from the realm of truth and of the true "I," to which such
striking reference had been made at the end of the course
of nineteen lessons. "In this School lies the potential core of
future development," Steiner had told Count Polzer.[293]

After meeting with Ita Wegman on January 27, 1935, two
months after her return and her outer and inner convalescence
in the Swiss mountains, Palestine, and Italy, Werner Pache
noted that she had spoken about the "spirit union and the
Christmas Foundation Meeting," and expressed her intention of "living in full faithfulness with these." She also said
she had decided to give Class lessons once again, but now in
free form, and had begun to do this.[294] Ita Wegman no longer
regarded the esoteric lessons she gave as being connected with
the Goetheanum, which had lost sight of the Christmas Foundation Meeting; she felt them to be entirely free of it—as an
"absolutely neutral spiritual asset."[295]

From that time on, therefore, she refused to hold Class
lessons at gatherings with any partisan Society emphasis and
sought to release the First Class fully from all Goetheanum
tensions and entanglements. In the remaining eight years of
her life, up to March 4, 1943, she held to this with absolute
consistency. In the situation as it was, she regarded this as the
only possible way forward; and at the same time she saw it
as an expression of a transitional period, trusting in a future

regeneration of the Goetheanum and the General Anthropo-sophical Society. She never relinquished this aim.[296]

On December 8, 1942, three months before her death, she held her last Class lesson in Arlesheim, the twelfth of the nineteen lessons, in which Steiner not only decisively furthers the developmental trajectory of his teaching, but also speaks in detail about meditation and ways of relating to the mantras:

> And we also ought...to acquire the inner mood of soul to feel that human self-knowledge is something festive, serious, sacred, and that these things ought only really to be spoken inwardly by the soul—let alone outwardly—in a way that allows us to feel them as something serious, festive, hallowed. That these things are spoken of so often in such a cliquish way can be a great obstacle to progressing further on an esoteric path if this serious, festive, hallowed mood is lacking; if, instead there is gossip about them with even, perhaps, a tinge of vanity. People forget that in esoteric life everything depends on truth prevailing—real, full truth. Without this awareness a person cannot get anywhere at all in esoteric life—without knowledge that truth, the full truth must hold sway there, and that one cannot therefore merely speak of truth yet still view things as they are viewed in mundane, outward life. This is what happens when people make these things a subject for ordinary gossip. And this ordinary gossip, which happens so frequently, casts a great many obstacles and hindrances upon the esoteric path. We must unite everything connected with self-knowledge with this serious, festive, hallowed mood in our soul.[297]

In the last three years of her life, still,[298] Ita Wegman made efforts to intensify the inner activity—her own and that of the Class community—of receiving and engaging with the lessons. After 1935, she herself had pursued a decisive path and in 1938 and '39 increasingly felt the wish and the need to leave Arlesheim and Dornach, to escape from the suffocating proximity of the Goetheanum and attempt a new beginning. The outbreak of World War II had prevented her from immigrating to Canada and founding a clinic there, as she had been considering. Eventually she went to Ascona, to Casa Andrea Cristoforo, intensifying the therapeutic and spiritual life there. She saw the risk of stagnation within a paralyzing, habitually repeated tradition, and also worked to strengthen the efficacy of the Class. "...In general it also seems to me that we all ought to be more inwardly active, so that the Class can work more effectively," she wrote in a letter in December in 1940, also saying that she did not wish to return to Arlesheim for a Class lesson.[299] She spoke of the need for "energetic further development" and of resurrection thoughts that she expected both of herself and of others ("first and foremost of myself"). She thought that this resurrection process ought also to affect the whole First Class, and must be accomplished through human consciousness, through a real inner path of development. "But a maturity must enter these efforts, so that the Class can attain a higher level through human beings. I am always working for this," she told Madeleine van Deventer in January 1941 in a letter from Ascona.[300] Ita Wegman was not primarily concerned with questions of form here but of consciousness.

Until December 8, 1942, she held the lessons in the wording by Rudolf Steiner, and with an inner stance she considered the only right and appropriate one toward Rudolf Steiner. Apart from the occult deed of the actual holding of the lessons, which she adhered to throughout her life, she had for many years strongly supported forms of study arising from independent engagement with the mantras, which she regarded as a real accompaniment, complement to, and support for the classes, although not as a substitute for them.[301] Ita Wegman did not surrender anything of the strength and full authority of the esoteric Class lessons in Steiner's wording, that is, the words coined by the initiate of the new mysteries. Rudolf Steiner's words had been recorded precisely in shorthand, were available in their precision, truth, and spiritual brilliance, and in certain circumstances he had agreed to their word-for-word rendition (for instance in the case of Lilly Kolisko and her lessons in Stuttgart for the faculty of teachers at the Waldorf school, or for the School members in Prague).[302]

But the question remained how those holding the lessons, and those receiving them could truly grow in consciousness toward their content. "Only when initiation is pursued with all its severe trials, may one be worthy to stand apart from the murder that holds sway at the Front," wrote Ita Wegman from Ascona to Arlesheim during the war years;[303] and this was the challenge for the community of Michaelites. Murder at the Front would not end in future either, in the age of the mystery of evil (Rudolf Steiner), but merely change its appearance.

If the First Class was really to become a vessel for the future regeneration of the General Anthroposophical Society, and especially of its School for Spiritual Science—in the form of its once intended spiritual core, from which all further essential development would have to proceed—then actual, successful initiation would be absolutely indispensable in times of war. The esoteric lessons had to be held with sufficient strength and presence of mind to enable Michael actually to be present in them, and they had to have the power to reach the depths of being of School members, and remind them of their incarnational resolve as Michaelites. Without any doubt this was a matter of the "I" growing apocalyptic, of which Rudolf Steiner spoke in his last lecture course to the priests of The Christian Community and the members of the esoteric executive council ("...so that your "I" becomes the sum of active powers that themselves are apocalyptic"[304])—and thus also of the real conquest of all habitual, bourgeois, cliquish tradition, but likewise of all casual uncommitted sensationalism. It was a matter of full responsibility in the face of the world situation, and toward the world of spirit, which was, as ever, bound up with the anthroposophic movement. "The effects of the Christmas Foundation Meeting should also include ever-developing clarity in the world, through members seeking to work actively, about what Anthroposophy essentially is *and is not*."[305]

Anticipating this in his poem "Responsibility," Rudolf Steiner's pupil, colleague and friend Christian Morgenstern had written in December 1912:

> We stand about here idly—
> while up above they wait for us!
> We merely walk here idly.
>
> No seriousness in our loyalty—
> while up above they wait for us:
> no serious, active loyalty.
>
> Neither above nor here below can grow
> from such poor help, meaning or victory.
> Above and below instead there grows
>
> from such half-heartedness shame and grief.
> The gods above are ailing and
> here human beings wither. Sorrow, grief
>
> replace the work of love within the world.[306]

Ita Wegman was not a melancholic person. In full knowledge of these conditions she was relying on the future, that is, on new generations of people who would uncompromisingly set about the work in the way Steiner had intended, and would also make the Class lessons into what they should have been from the beginning. In one of his words of guidance during a lesson, Rudolf Steiner had said: "For a movement rooted in the spirit, my dear friends, it really is not a matter of how many members it has, but about the strength at work in it from the world of spirit."[307]

The Michaelic substance requires our protection, our enveloping care that, as true, faithful pupils of Michael we can only give it ourselves in our souls, individually and as a community of human beings called upon to do so. (Sergei O. Prokofieff)[308]

> *Be in time and eternity*
> *Pupils in the light of Michael*
> *In the love of gods*
> *In the heights of the cosmos*[309]

Appendix

The Ritual of Admission into Joint Leadership of the Michael School [310]

The soul's fruits
They ripen for me
When I can send
To you in spirit
An earthly countenance.

To me appears then
Past existence
In the fire
Rejoicing
To create a form
That wraps me round
In the spirits' house.

So take the hand of soul
Which my I—yours—
Extends to you
And undertake what I desire.

What is undertaken then will be
As though my own self
Wrote the script.

Rudolf Steiner for Ita Wegman [311]

Rudolf Steiner's Rose Cross (front)

Just five months after Rudolf Steiner's death, on August 21, 1925, in a letter to Albert Steffen about her relationship to the First Class of the School, Ita Wegman wrote of a rose cross that Steiner had given to her: "Before his illness, and following a ritual enactment we performed together, the Doctor himself placed around my neck a small cross with small rubies clasped in roses, that he had worn around his neck on a red ribbon."[312] Rudolf Steiner's rose cross is included in Ita Wegman's estate.[313] A few years later, on April 25, 1930, at a meeting of the executive council at the Goetheanum with general secretaries and delegates of the General Anthroposophical Society, Wegman spoke in more detail about this gift of the cross and the preceding ritual enactment, as well as its relationship to the First Class: *"And he also directly gave me his cross, which he removed from around his neck and, with his own hands, placed around mine, saying, 'From this moment onward we are both there for the Michael School together.'"[314]*

Accordingly, following a ritual enactment, Rudolf Steiner admitted Ita Wegman to joint responsibility for, or joint leadership of the Michael School, by the rite of giving her the cross. No record exists of when this occurred. Wegman gave no date, but told Steffen in her letter that it was "before his illness," which became apparent at the end of September 1924. It seems very likely that Steiner performed the ritual act and gave Wegman the cross at the beginning of that month in his studio, after his return from England; for in all Class lessons he gave from September 6 onward in Dornach, he emphasized Ita Wegman's joint responsibility for the mantras of these cultic lessons or for the esoteric School. From now on, too, during September 1924, Steiner and Wegman together ritually inducted those who were admitted to the First Class.

≈

No more was known for many decades about the gift of the rose cross and especially about the rite that preceded it although both occurrences—quite clearly belonging together—are of great importance also for the Class lessons themselves, in which first cultic elements were included from the end of August 1924 (the sign and seal of Michael. It is clear from an unpublished meeting transcript of November 29, 1930, that Ita Wegman possessed a written record of the cultic enactment that had been performed. Compelled by the new crisis in the executive council and the Society to explain to her colleagues that Rudolf Steiner had transferred to her a shared responsibility for the Class (which no one apart from Elisabeth Vreede believed), Wegman said in relation to the ritual act "I will bring with me papers [tomorrow] with the precise words that he [Dr. Steiner] actually said to me. I will read out the words he spoke in this ritual."[315] It is not recorded whether Ita Wegman in fact did this on November 30, 1930.

Ita Wegman spoke of the shared enactment of a rite, an act that concluded with the handing to her of the rose cross. The papers in which the cultic enactment or aspects of it were recorded belonged to an extensive collection of mantras and esoteric exercises in Steiner's handwriting that she preserved. The collection is still extant in its entirety, and was published in 2009 by the priest Emanuel Zeylmans van Emmicho-ven.[316] It includes a text of several pages (in the handwriting of Rudolf Steiner and Ita Wegman) that focuses on the rose cross and the giving of it to Wegman, culminating with the latter and revealing cultic-ritual elements in the interplay of two people.

Emanuel Zeylmans van Emmichoven wrote, "Because Ita Wegman noted Rudolf Steiner's verbal comments, it is possible to get a sense of the detailed images and personal indications in the text."[317] There can be little doubt, now that we know about the contexts described above, that the transcripts record or contain the cultic ritual that Rudolf Steiner accomplished with Ita Wegman in the late summer of 1924.[318] The whole text comprised an evening and morning meditation for Ita Wegman, both culminating in the encounter with a priest-like figure and the giving of a rose cross; the mantric contents are connected with the path of schooling of the First Class and end with a blessing to the meditant who receives the rose cross from the priest figure—the *spirit guide.* We can only conjecture how much of this whole text was spoken during the ritual enactment in Rudolf Steiner's studio. It is very likely, however, that it included at least the intertwined words centered on the Rose Cross and the concluding, ritual blessing.

≈

The evening meditation exercise for Ita Wegman begins with the *ruckschau,* the review of an event during the day ("picture an event of the day in reverse"[319]). This is followed, in her own transcript containing precise instructions from Rudolf Steiner, by a breathing exercise that is repeated seven times, an IAO exercise, and then the Imagination of the Rose Cross. Clearly this imagination should be connected with a mantra related to the spiritual human form, in other words one that should be meditated on in relation to this form (centered on the heart and limb system[320]):

> Primal powers uphold me
> Spirits of fire free me
> Spirits of light illumine me
> So that I reach toward spiritual existence
> So that I feel soul beings
> So that I step over uncertainties
> So that I stand over abysses

Deepened in this way, the Rose Cross meditation implies a strengthening and sustaining of the human being in the heart region (out of the powers of the third hierarchy) so as to gain inner certainty and prove equal to tasks and dangers faced on behalf of humanity.

After this elevation, strengthening, and empowerment (or encouragement) of the human being, inner centering should follow—deep contemplation of the Christ mystery within one's own being,[321] based on these mantric words:

> In me may Christ live
> And transform my breath
> And warm the course of my blood
> And shine into my soul being.

The evening meditation ends with the instruction "abiding tranquil within oneself." In the margin of the page, following a square bracket, Rudolf Steiner wrote: "white robe. Red belt and / pendant. Red headband. / I: *Ave frater* / He: *rosae et aureae* / I: *crucis* / He: *Benedictus deus qui dedit / nobis signum.*"

The transcript that Rudolf Steiner gave Ita Wegman was very clearly a summary as aide memoire. Verbally he elaborated the inner process for her a good deal further. As she noted, after the Christ meditation, the Rose Cross had to be drawn forth again from the meditant's heart into which it had previously been laid. Wegman did not record whether the Imagination of the Rose Cross (based on the mantric verse "Primal powers uphold me ... ") should be experienced as the spiritual *forming* of a Rose Cross (and its storing in the central human organ of the heart). But the trajectory of the whole indicates that the Rose Cross had to be mantrically created or recreated in the exercise, and internalized.

The Rose Cross drawn forth from the heart was then, step by step to be borne up imaginatively upon a mountain. At its summit was to take place the encounter with a figure (person) in a priestly robe (with white cloak, red stola, red ribbon around his neck, and red belt, the *white–red* colors of Christian Rosenkreutz in *The Chymical Wedding*). In relation to this encounter, Wegman wrote:

> One gives the Rose Cross to this person and says to him: *"Ave frater"* [greetings, brother]. One feels that the other replies: *"Rosae et aureae"* [of the pink and golden-colored]. One replies with devotion: *"Crucis"* [cross]. The other says, *"Benedictus deus qui dedit nobis signum"* [Blessed be God who gave us the sign].

The imaginatively experienced encounter, that is, speaking together—by *intertwining* its meaning—the sentence, "Greetings, brother / of the pink- and rose-colored / cross," is followed by the thanks to God from the priestly figure and the giving of the Rose Cross that has been carried aloft; and then the meditant descends again: "Then the fiurther Imagination that one is departing from this other. At this, let tranquility enter the soul, and empty your consciousness." The Rose Cross remains on the mountain.

≈

As a memory aid for the morning meditation, Rudolf Steiner wrote down only the following:

> Imagination on the mountain. Being received.
> Holding up ♰

> My head harden universal spirit
> Free thought-light's life therefrom
> My larynx wither the soul of breezes
> Pour into it sense of spirit words
> My *heart* be inhabited by you my spirit guide
> Unite me with you
> So that I float live weave in spirit-soul existence

Ita Wegman noted in more detail:

> In the morning imagine that one has climbed the mountain again, and meets the same person with the same robe, and that this person gives back the Rose Cross that one gave him the evening before. Imagine that one meditates the following while kneeling:

> 1. My head harden universal spirit
>   Free thought-light's life therefrom
> 2. My larynx wither the soul of breezes
>   Pour into it sense of spirit words
>   My *heart* be inhabited by you my spirit guide
> 3. Unite me with you
>   So that I float live weave in spirit-soul existence!

> 1. Feel the head—thinking—like a stone
> 2. The larynx like a withered plant
> 3. Concentration on the heart while meditating the above

> Now one should meditate that this person who returns the Rose Cross places his right hand on his left then places both hands on the [other's] forehead and speaks the following words: *"Benedictus deus qui dedit nobis signum."*

Again empty your mind.

The meditation of the pupil once more walking on the mountain, accomplished in kneeling, thus culminates in spiritual union with the priestly other, becoming one in the heart, the destined organ of the Rose Cross ("My *heart* be inhabited by you my spirit guide / Unite me with you.") Following this, it appears from Wegman's transcript, the spirit guide hands over (or gives back) the Rose Cross to the pupil, along with a form of blessing by placing his hands on the pupil's head.

≈

"...I received his cross...directly from him: he removed it from around his neck and gave it to me, saying, *'From this moment onward we are both present together for the Michael School,'*" wrote Wegman about the moment when Rudolf Steiner handed her the cross, directly after the cultic ritual had been performed. Rudolf Steiner wished to work with Wegman for the Michael School "in unified work of soul,"[322] that is, spiritually united or one ("Unite me with you"), accompanying and supporting her on her inner path, but also needing her help.[323]

"My *heart* be inhabited by you my spirit guide / Unite me with you / So that I float live weave in spirit-soul existence!" were the last lines of the mantra that the pupil was to meditate, in imagined kneeling, directly before she received the Rose Cross. In the sign of this cross and its wearer, Rudolf Steiner and Ita Wegman remained united until March 29 1925, and meditated together each day: "Christian Rosenkreutz plays a great part in these meditations..." (Ita Wegman).[324]

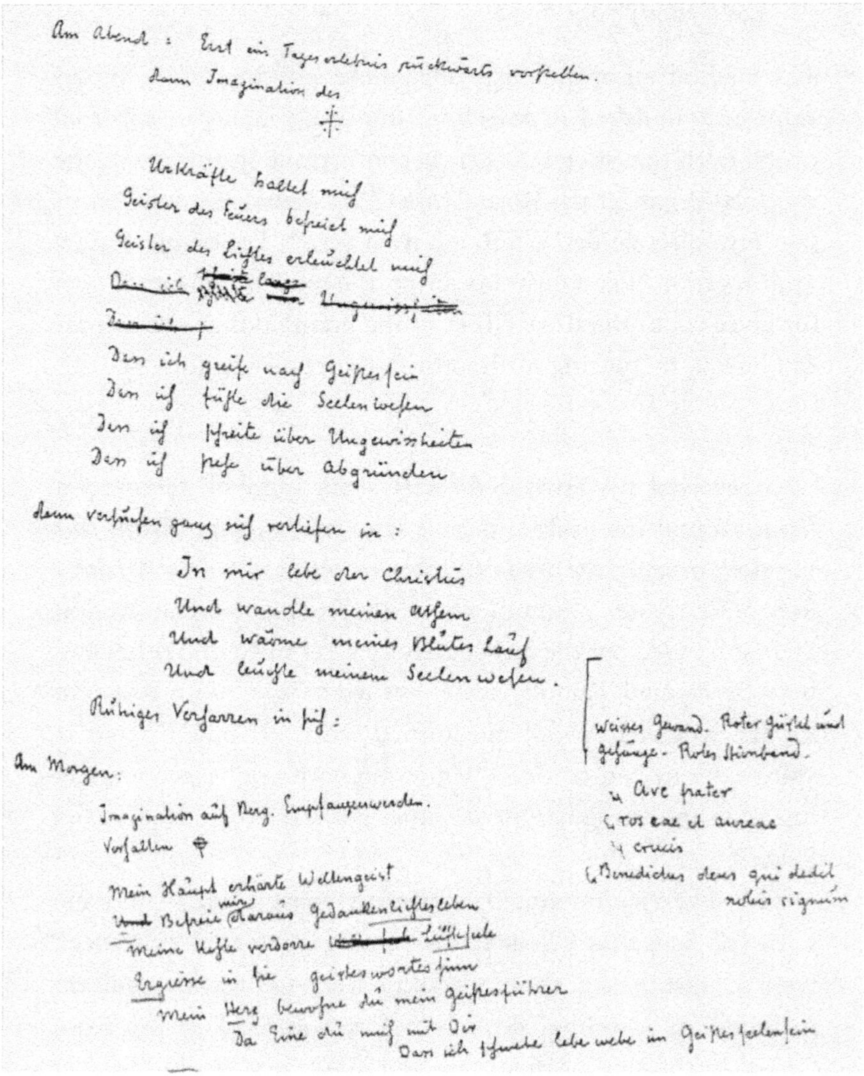
Am Abend: Erst ein Tageserlebnis rückwärts vorstellen.
Dann Imagination des

Urkräfte haltet mich
Geister des Feuers befreiet mich
Geister des Lichtes erleuchtet mich
~~Denn ich [illegible] lange [illegible] Ungewissheiten~~
~~Denn ich~~
Dass ich greife nach Geistessein
Dass ich fühle die Seelenwesen
Dass ich schreite über Ungewissheiten
Dass ich stehe über Abgründen

Dann versuchen ganz sich vertiefen in:
In mir lebe der Christus
Und wandle meinen Athem
Und wärme meines Blutes Lauf
Und leuchte meinem Seelenwesen.

Ruhiges Verharren in sich:

Weisses Gewand. Roter Gürtel und Gehänge. Rotes Stirnband.

Ave frater
Roseae et aureae
crucis
Benedictus deus qui dedit nobis signum

Am Morgen:
Imagination auf Berg. Empfangenwerden.
Vorstellen
Mein Haupt erhärte Weltengeist
~~Und~~ Befreie mir daraus Gedankenlichtesleben
Meine Kehle verdorre ~~[illegible]~~ Lichtseele
Ergiesse in sie Geisteswortessinn
Mein Herz bewohne du mein Geistesführer
Da Eine du mich mit Dir
Dass ich schwebe lebe webe in Geistesseelensein

Meditation instructions in Rudolf Steiner's handwriting

Meditation

Am Abend Rückschau
über das am Tage vorge-
fallene in Bilderform
Einen tiefen Atemzug holen
dieser Atem dann gehen lassen
vom Nasenwurzel über das
Haupt bis zum hinteren Teil
des Nackens (J)
Den Atem halten dann gehen
lassen vom Nacken durch
die Ärme in die Handpalme
(A) Rechter Handpalm auf
das linke (O) dann den
Atemzug durch den Solar
Plexus gehen lassen.
(7 Malen wiederholen)

Transcript in Ita Wegman's handwriting

1

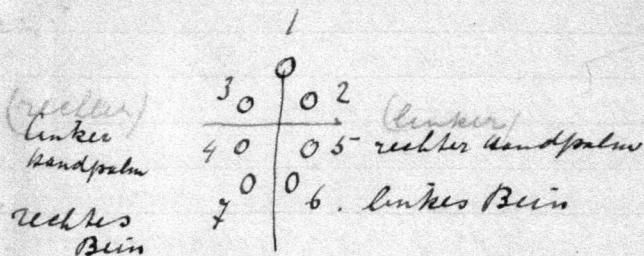

(reeller)
linker
Handpalm

rechtes
Bein

    3 0   0 2
    4 0   0 5 – rechter Handpalm (linker)
       0   0 6. linkes Bein
    7   6. linkes Bein

1-2-3
Herz 1) Urkräfte haltet mich
archa 2) Geister des Feuers befeuert mich
angel 3) Geister des Lichts erleuchtet mich
     4) Dass ich greife nach
                Geisteswesen
     5) Dass ich fühle die Seelenwesen
     6) Dass ich schreite über Enge,
              wie heiten
     7) Dass ich stehe über Abgründen

Dann meditieren die Worte
    In mir lebe der Christus
    Und wandle meinen Atem
    Und leuchte meinen Seelenwesen

nach dieser Meditation das

Rosenkreuz aus dem Herzen
in dem man er vorher gelegt
hat heraus holen
Daraufhin muss man die
Imagination haben das
man Schritt für Schritt
zu einem Berg hinaufsteigt
den Rosenkreuz tragend.
Auf der Bergspitze begegnet
man eine Person in einem
weissen Gewand mit roten
Stola, roten Gurt und roten
Band um dem Hals
An diesen Person gibt man
den Rosenkreuz und sagt
zu ihm „Ave frater"
Man fühlt, dass der andere
antwortet „Rosae et aurae
man antwortet mit devotion
zurück. Crucis"
Der andere sagt: „Benedictus
Deus qui dedit nobis Signum
        qui

Dann die weitere Imagination
dass man diesen andern
verlässt
Daraufhin Ruhe eintreten
lassen in der Seele
Leer machen das Bewußtsein
—

Morgens imaginieren:
dass man wieder den Berg
aufgestiegen ist, dass man
die gleiche Person mit der
gleichen Gewandung begegnet
und dass diese das Rosen-
kreuz wieder zurückgibt
das man ihm den vorigen
Abend gegeben hat
Imaginieren, dass man
knieend das folgende medit..
1) Mein Haupt erhärte Weltengeist
Befeure mir daraus Gedankenhelleslebe
2) Meine Kehle verdorre Lüfteseele
Ergiesse in sie Geisteswortesinn
3) Mein Herz bewohne du mein Geistesfüh..
Da eine Du mich mit Dir
Dass ich schwebe lebe webe in Geistes..
, seelensein!

der denken

1) Fühlen das Haupt (wie ein
Stein

2) Die Kehle wie eine verdorrte
Pflanze

3) Concentration auf das Herz
bei der meditation des
vorangegangenen

—

Nun ist zu meditieren
dass diese Person den Rosen
kreuz zurückgibt, dass
er die rechte Hand auf der
linken legt, dass beide Hände
auf die Stirn legt und die
folgenden Worte spricht:
„Benedictus Deus qui dedit
nobis signum"
wieder leeres Bewustsein
machen

The Relationship with the School

Teachers, physicians, and priests in 1924 [325]

In whatever field, we must always and everywhere embody the full truth as representatives of the being of Anthroposophy in the world; and we must be aware that in so far as we are unable to do this, we cannot in fact support and cultivate the anthroposophic movement. Veiled commitment to the anthroposophic movement ultimately leads, you see, to nothing beneficial.

RUDOLF STEINER, Dec. 24, 1923 [326]

/7

Liebe Freunde !

Unseren , einem Versprechen gleichkommenden Mitteilungen
über die Führung der medizinischen Sektion am Goetheanum , die wir gele-
gentlich der Weihnachtstagung gemacht haben , nachkommend , senden wir
war an die für die Pflege des Medizinischen mit uns Verbundenen diesen
ersten Rundbrief : Er ist getragen von der Gesinnung , die uns bei den
den medizinischen Kursen im Neujahr vereinte : Er möchte am liebsten
jedem Worte etwas mitgeben von den Gefühlen für die leidende Menschheit,
aus dem allein nicht nur die Hingabe an die Heilkunst , sondern auch deren wirkliche Kraft hervorgehen muss :

Es war in alten Zeiten,
Da lebte in der Eingeweihten Seelen
Kraftvoll der Gedanke, dass krank
Von Natur ein jeglicher Mensch sei;
Und Erziehen ward angesehen
Gleich dem Heilprozess ,
Der dem Kinde mit dem Reifen
Die Gesundheit zugleich erbrachte
Für des Lebens vollendetes Menschsein .

Es ist gut, solch kraftvolle Gedanken , gewonnen aus der Anschauung alter
instinktiver Weisheit , sich vor die Seele treten zu lassen , wenn man
in rechter innerlicher Sammlung die Seele bereiten will , zum Erfassen
der Heileswirkungen : VERGESSEN

Vergessen wir nicht , dass dem Heilprozesse eine Seele
mitgegeben werden muss , da er nicht nur an einen Körper , sondern
auch an eine Seele sich wenden muss : Je mehr solche Gedanken die jungen
Aerzte begreifen , desto mehr wird in das medizinische Leben das einflies-
sen , was der sinnige Arzt sehnsüchtig verlangt , wenn er den heutigen
Stand seiner Kunst mit den Grenzen empfindet , was der Kranke wie eine
Gnade empfinden wird , wenn er es im Heilprozesse erlebt :

Liebe Freunde , Ihr habt , so weit Ihr im Januar hier ver-
sammelt wart , offenen Herzens entgegengenommen , was aus solcher Gesinnung an Euch herantreten wollte : Uns wird unvergesslich sein , wie aus
Euern Augen dies gesprochen , aus Euern warmen Worten dies zu uns gedrun-
gen ist : Unsere Gedanken weilten bei Euch , und sie sollen heute zum
ersten Male in Anknüpfung an Eure gestellten Fragen zu Euch hinwandeln :

Wir senden das Folgende an einzelne Adressen und bitten
diejenigen, die von uns direkte Sendung erhalten , dafür zu sorgen , dass
sie weiter gehen an die von uns mitgeteilten Adressen :

*Rudolf Steiner/Ita Wegman: newsletter for the young doctors,
page 1. Dornach March 11, 1924
(© Ita Wegman Archive, Arlesheim)*

In their first meeting after the Christmas Foundation Meeting and founding of the School, the faculty of Stuttgart Waldorf teachers approached Rudolf Steiner with questions relating to the future relationship between their school, the Goetheanum and the School for Spiritual Science. At this meeting, which took place in Stuttgart on February 5, 1924, ten days before the first Class lesson, Rudolf Steiner made clear from the beginning that, for reasons also relating to the school's public profile, he did not favor a direct affiliation of the Free Waldorf School with the School in Dornach, though the teaching faculty as such ought indeed to join the School, *"or those individuals within the faculty who wish this not only for themselves personally but as teachers at the School."* [327] A living relationship of this kind arising through joining the School, which would make it possible to mediate the impulses from Dornach to the school, was something Steiner regarded as desirable and necessary:

> The difference [from the status quo] would be that the relationship so far to anthroposophic pedagogy has been more theoretical, but that in future it would be a more living one in which, either as a whole faculty or as individuals, people would orient themselves to impulses arising when, as a teacher at the Free Waldorf School, one is a member of the School for Spiritual Science. [328]

At the time of the conversation—just five weeks after the Christmas Foundation Meeting—most of the teachers in Stuttgart had already sought admission to the First Class, writing to Rudolf Steiner in Dornach to apply. In the meeting he made it clear that it was, firstly, desirable and useful for all teachers to join a School that, "basically, would work to cultivate insight and life," and where the individual could engage in

"learning in and for itself," at the same time working successfully—as a university—actually to fulfill scientific and artistic
tasks;[329] but he also stressed the importance of teachers joining the School not only as individual people on their own path
of schooling, but in their capacity as teachers at the *Stuttgart
Waldorf School.* In this context he asked:

> Are the teachers at the school satisfied to belong to the
> School of Spiritual Science in Dornach as individuals,
> or do they seek to become members as a faculty so that
> each person joining does so in the capacity of a teacher
> at the Waldorf School? In doing the latter, the teachers
> will require the Pedagogical Section in Dornach to con-
> cern itself with the Waldorf School, whereas otherwise it
> will only address pedagogy in a more general sense. There
> really is a big difference here.[330]

It was clear which of the two options Steiner favored (and
from a spiritual perspective *had to* favor).

When Lili Kolisko asked him soon after this in Dornach
to be allowed to take down the Class lessons in shorthand so
as to present them to anthroposophists in Stuttgart, Steiner
allowed it, requesting however that this not be to any group
of anthroposophists but specifically to the *faculty of teachers*
at the Waldorf School in Stuttgart, with whom he wished to
work esoterically. ("At this Dr. Steiner continued, 'Would you
not wish to convey this to the faculty of Waldorf teachers?'
Naturally, I was very willing to do so, and Dr. Steiner prom-
ised to issue [School] membership cards for the whole faculty
immediately."[331])

The Stuttgart teachers' faculty had taken up the suggestion
proposed and explained by Steiner in the meeting of February 5, 1924. This was the right and sensible direction to go

in—the Dornach School wished and needed to become active and productive in specialist fields, which included pedagogy. Membership of the Dornach School was not just a question of one's personal path of schooling but the basic premise for the Christmas Foundation Meeting's impulses to become effective within this School. The teacher's faculty could become an esoteric organ (*"The faculty should form a core from which something can then emanate"*[332]).

Subsequently the Class lessons were held by Lili Kolisko for the community of teachers, and became a sustaining substance for the faculty.[333] This was not the only innovation. For the first time, both The Executive Council of the [General] Anthroposophical Society and The Faculty of Teachers of the Free Waldorf School carried *joint* responsibility for the public education conference organized by the Stuttgart Waldorf School ("The Place of Education in Personal and Cultural Life Today" [Apr. 7–13, 1924]).[334]

The conference's program and aims, which Rudolf Steiner himself formulated, were presented by him for the agreement of all colleagues on the exoteric executive council in Dornach ("for perusal by and signed agreement of the executive council"). Steiner signed it first, followed by Albert Steffen, Ita Wegman, Marie Steiner, Guenther Wachsmuth, and Elisabeth Vreede.[335] This marked the beginning of a new era for the Waldorf School, or the faculty of teachers, in their collaboration with Rudolf Steiner and connection with the Dornach School.

≈

The situation among the physicians was a great deal more complex, since this group was not a community, and anything other than homogenous. Medical work was extremely diverse in nature—in clinics and practices at various places and with different tasks, conditions, and aims.[336] Many affiliated themselves with the School in Dornach on an individual basis as and when they sought this. But of particular interest for an understanding of the situation after the Christmas Foundation Meeting and for Rudolf Steiner's intentions with the School, were the occurrences within the group of young doctors, an initially loose association of medical students and junior physicians. Dissatisfied with the middle-class tendencies of anthroposophic physicians, and enthusiastic about a spirit of innovation and the search for a real humanization of medicine, they had first approached Steiner in the fall of 1922.[337]

In January and April 1924, these medical students and physicians received special courses from Rudolf Steiner, the first School courses after the Christmas Foundation Meeting. These had an esoteric–mantric structure and were held fully in the spirit of the Class lessons, but in a specific professional field.[338] Although most of his audience were extremely young, did not all belong to the Anthroposophical Society and by no means all envisaged applying to join the Dornach School, Rudolf Steiner, *on his own initiative,* admitted them to the School as a whole young doctors group before the start of the Easter course. Madeleine van Deventer wrote in a memoir:

"It seems to me important to mention that immediately on our arrival in Dornach we received our First Class membership certificate. This was accorded even to those who had not yet submitted a request for it."[339] There is also documentary proof that, in the Class lesson held on Good Friday, April 18, 1924, Rudolf Steiner spoke of his March 11 newsletter to the group of young doctors as a communication to Class members—*from the work of the School*—although, at the time the newsletter was composed, the group had not yet been admitted to the School. (This happened only shortly before the Class lesson.) School members were in future to be informed through these newsletters about the ongoing work of the School in professional disciplines,[340] and about what "flows through this School itself in Dornach."[341] Steiner made a beginning with this in his medical newsletter of March 11, 1924—in answer to questions that he and Ita Wegman had received after the January course. The newsletter begins with the sentence:

> In fulfillment of what, tantamount to a promise, we stated during the Christmas Foundation Meeting about leadership of the Medical Section at the Goetheanum, we are sending out this, our first newsletter for those connected with us in nurturing medicine. This newsletter is sustained by the outlook that also united us during our medical courses in the New Year.[342]

Rudolf Steiner and Ita Wegman spoke of the already existing connection with the School and its Medical Section, created by the course and intrinsically esoteric in nature ("...for those *connected with us* in nurturing medicine..."). The course in January 1924 formed a first esoteric and exoteric course of instruction by the Medical Section at the Goetheanum, and was part of this Section's developmental process as the medical department of the new School. Participants were not only to attend lectures and assimilate them individually, but, in accord with the Dornach impulse, work together as a community. Rudolf Steiner spoke of the group's federation as an affiliation with Dornach—a connection *"among you with us here"*—and said of the fundamentally new situation or new beginning for the anthroposophic movement after the Christmas Foundation Meeting:

> From this moment on... a kind of radical change must arise in our whole view of the anthroposophic movement, also in specific fields. As you begin to seek your path in medicine, you must from the outset inwardly participate in this real change. You see, in pursuing the esoteric path it cannot be a matter of mere addition or supplement but rather a complete imbuing of our path in life with esoteric impulses. [343]

Implicit here was a view of the School as a real center of research and teaching, and in this context affiliation with Dornach was necessary and useful for the young doctors without exception. Steiner regarded the spiritual, initiate-level work in the Sections accomplished in Dornach as belonging to the esoteric School itself; and professional groups, participating in and sharing responsibility for this, must naturally belong to it. From the group of young doctors—as a medical Class community—the esoteric core of the Medical Section eventually also developed, and with this Rudolf Steiner wished to initiate a new medical Mystery schooling, further cultivating and elaborating the Medical Section in this way. His illness and death prevented this happening. [344]

≈

In a reminiscence, Gottfried Husemann wrote as follows about the relationship between the priests of The Christian Community and the Dornach School, and the last Apocalypse course given in Dornach in September 1924:

> *"I will admit you all to the First Class of the School for Spiritual Science,"* he [Steiner] said as he greeted us. This

was done in the following days, and thus the priests, besides attending the Apocalypse lectures and the evening sessions [the karma lectures] were also able to participate in the first course of the Michael School. *"You will also,"* he added, *"receive newsletters from the School."* This never came about. *"Relationships with the anthroposophic movement will become ever more inward."*[345]

Like the teachers of the Stuttgart school, various priests of The Christian Community had, in February 1924, discussed with Rudolf Steiner its relationship with the general Anthroposophical Society and the newly founded School in Dornach. At this stage, already, Steiner had affirmed intensifying collaboration, and Class admission, and spoken of his intention to send out School newsletters in future. He made a first beginning with this in March (with Ita Wegman) for the physicians. However, he did not seek to establish a Theological Section in Dornach, instead advocating continuation of the work of research, teaching, and cultic practice that the movement for religious renewal had developed in Stuttgart since the fall of 1922. However, he emphatically supported the active participation of priests in the new developments in Dornach, both individually and as an esoteric community. In September 1924, as with the young doctors six months earlier, but in this case at the request of Friedrich Rittelmeyer, Rudolf Steiner facilitated School admission also to priests who had not yet been members of the Anthroposophical Society for two years, or who even did not belong to it at all. In a meeting in Stuttgart in June 1924, he told Waldorf teachers:

> You must not forget that the priests of The Christian Community are among those anthroposophists who have made the greatest progress in the shortest time. The priests are not the same people they were; they have made huge

advances in their inner development. In the short time the movement has existed, they have shown exemplary development in their whole life of soul. Not all of them, of course, but by and large this is true, and in all areas of life they exert a blessed influence.[346]

In the Apocalypse course, in September 1924, finally, Rudolf Steiner spoke about *"what can make The Christian Community into the bearer of a key part of the new mysteries"*;[347] and thus indirectly addressed the intrinsic connection between the movement for religious renewal, with its content and aims, and the Dornach School. Elsewhere, six months previously, he had spoken as follows about the mission of the School in a general lecture on Anthroposophy:

> The mysteries themselves faded at a time when the free development of the human being had to come to the fore. Now the time has come when the mysteries must be rediscovered. They must be rediscovered. We must be fully aware of the fact that efforts must be made today to find the mysteries once again. It is in this awareness that we held the Christmas Foundation Meeting, for it is urgently necessary to have a place on Earth where the mysteries can be established once more. The Anthroposophical Society, as it evolves, must become the path to the renewed mysteries.[348]

Historical evidence shows the importance Rudolf Steiner assigned to an inner sense of affiliation with the School, not just on an individual basis but also for communities of people whose specific professional tasks were part of the Dornach School's effective work within, and influence upon, civilization. What was "really intended by the Goetheanum for the evolution of the world and civilization"[349] could only enter the world through esoterically connected people who embraced

Dornach and its spirituality, and were willing and ready to represent this spirituality courageously, both its methodology and its content, in specific professional fields of practice in the world: "I am there as a representative of the Anthroposophy that issues from and originates at the Goetheanum."[350]

Notes and References

1   Rudolf Steiner, *Esoterische Unterweisungen für die erste Klasse der Freien Hochschule für Geisteswissenschaft am Goetheanum* (1924). CW 270a, 2008, p. 124.

2   Peter Selg, *Rudolf Steiner and the School for Spiritual Science: The Foundation of the "First Class,"* SteinerBooks 2012.

3   Cf. Johannes Kiersch, *Zur Entwicklung der Freien Hochschule für Geisteswissenschaft. Die Erste Klasse.* Dornach 2005 (new expanded edition entitled *Steiners individualisierte Esoterik einst und jetzt. Zur Entwicklung der Freien Hochschule für Geisteswissenschaft.* Dornach 2012). [The first edition is published in English as: *A History of the School of Spiritual Science: The First Class*, Temple Lodge 2006.]

4   Cf. Peter Selg, *Rudolf Steiner und die Freie Hochschule für Geisteswissenschaft. Die Begründung der "Ersten Klasse,"* Arlesheim 2008, pp. 14ff. [In English: *Rudolf Steiner and the School for Spiritual Science: The Foundation of the "First Class,"* SteinerBooks 2012.]

5   Guenther Roeschert, "Restauration und Innovation. Die Hochschule entwickelt sich aus freien Forschungsgemeinschaften und nicht aus 'Verwirklichung der Schrift.'" In *Das Goetheanum*, No. 37, 15 December 2012, p. 20.

6   Johannes Kiersch, in Lydia Fechner, "Spirituelle Identität zwischen Abgrenzung und Offenheit. Die Redaktion im Gespräch mit Johannes Kiersch und Günther Röschert." In *Die Drei* 6/2014, p. 112.

7   Quoted in Johannes Kiersch, *Steiners individualisierte Esoterik einst und jetzt. Zur Entwicklung der Freien Hochschule für Geisteswissenschaft.* Dornach 2012, p. 331. [First edition in English: *A History of the School of Spiritual Science: The First Class*, Temple Lodge 2006.]

8   Ibid., p. 190.

9   Rudolf Steiner, *Anthroposophische Leitsätze. Der Erkenntnisweg der Anthroposophie—Das Michael-Mysterium.* CW 26. Dornach 1998, p. 102. [In English: *Anthroposophical Leading Thoughts*, Rudolf Steiner Press 2001.]

10   In relation to questions surrounding the publication of the Class
      texts, as well as other matters, Jørgen Smit examined the nature of
      the ahrimanic attack arising from the "materialistic influence" or
      having there, at least, its very greatest scope for attack. ("And thus
      we must also regard undesired publication as a campaign by ahri-
      manic powers to render things more superficial and external.") In
      relation to the other pole of anti-Christian influence he continued
      by saying, "The other danger, one that has continually increased in
      recent years, is that of numerous occultist streams in close proxim-
      ity to the Anthroposophical Society and actually also penetrating
      it. There are already a couple of dozen of these diverse streams,
      not even working together, and yet sharing a common trait which
      is to gain access as swiftly as possible to spiritual experiences and
      spiritual influences. They wish to do this without embarking on
      the arduous path of knowledge, self-knowledge, world knowledge,
      leading to the Guardian of the Threshold and to the crossing of
      this threshold, which requires us to rise to direct spirit knowledge
      through configuring thinking within the consciousness soul. They
      seek to avoid this hard work and difficulty and reach spiritual
      experience without such effort, guided by some guru or currently,
      in several occultist movements close to the Anthroposophical Soci-
      ety, to do so via female figures who take the lead in this respect.
      Being drawn in this way into occultist experiences devoid of the
      consciousness soul, overleaping this serious, arduous, difficult
      path of knowledge, involves a great danger to the realization of the
      Michael School on Earth. The Michael School in the world of spirit
      is not at risk from this. It is sovereign and secure both in respect of
      luciferic and ahrimanic powers. But on Earth, in human hearts, a
      battle is being waged." (In Johannes Kiersch, *Steiners individual-
      isierte Esoterik einst und jetzt. Zur Entwicklung der Freien Hoch-
      schule für Geisteswissenschaft*, pp. 354f.) [This quotation is not
      contained in the earlier English edition: *A History of the School of
      Spiritual Science: The First Class*, Temple Lodge 2006.]

11   Ibid., p. 354.

12   Ibid., p. 356.

13   Sergei O. Prokofieff, *Die Erste Klasse der Michael-Schule und ihre
      christologischen Grundlagen*. Dornach 2009, p. 460 (for Class
      members) [In English: *The First Class of the Michael School and
      Its Christological Foundations*, Dornach 2012.]

14   Rudolf Steiner to Count Ludwig Polzer-Hoditz, Nov. 11, 1924. In
      Thomas Meyer, *Ludwig Polzer-Hoditz. Ein Europäer*. Basel 2008,

p. 666. [In English: T. H. Meyer, *Ludwig Polzer-Hoditz: A European*, Temple Lodge 2014.]

15 Ita Wegman, Letter to Anna Gunnarsson Wager, October 16, 1924. Ita Wegman Archive, Arlesheim.

16 Rudolf Steiner, *Vorstufen zum Mysterium von Golgotha.* CW 152. Dornach 1990, p. 44.

17 Rudolf Steiner, Esoterische Unterweisungen *für die erste Klasse der Freien Hochschule für Geisteswissenschaft am Goetheanum 1924.* CW 270a, Dornach 2008, p. 1.

18 Cf. Rudolf Steiner, *The Reappearance of Christ in the Etheric*, CW 118; and Sergei O. Prokofieff, *The Appearance of Christ in the Etheric: Spiritual-Scientific Aspects of the Second Coming*, Temple Lodge 2012.

19 Rudolf Steiner, *Four Mystery Plays*, CW 14, and Peter Selg, *Esoterische Gemeinschaften in Rudolf Steiners Mysteriendramen*, Arlesheim 2010.

20 Rudolf Steiner, *Occult History—Historical Personalities and Events in the Light of Spiritual Science*, CW 126. The title of Steiner's lecture course at the Christmas Foundation Meeting in 1923/24: "World History in the Light of Anthroposophy, and as Foundation of Knowledge of the Human Spirit"—intentionally related to the title of the course in Stuttgart, to which he expressly and repeatedly referred (eight times altogether). Cf. Peter Selg, "Rudolf Steiners Abendvorträge der Weihnachtstagung," in Peter Selg and Marc Desaules (ed.), *Die Sozialgestalt der Weihnachtstagung,* Arlesheim 2014, pp. 89ff. As Friedrich Hiebel told Sergei O. Prolofieff, Steiner placed the large format typescript edition of the course on "Occult History" (which he had given in 1912) on his lectern during the evening lectures at the Christmas Foundation Meeting.

21 Rudolf Steiner, *An Occult Physiology*, CW 128, Rudolf Steiner Press 1997. Steiner entitled this course "Occult Physiology" and not "*An* Occult Physiology," clearly with reference to *Occult History.*

22 Cf. Peter Selg, *Rudolf Steiner (1861–1925). Lebens- und Werkgeschichte*, vol. 2. Arlesheim 2012, pp. 1196ff.

23 Rudolf Steiner, CW 15.

24 Rudolf Steiner, *Das esoterische Christentum und die geistige Führung der Menschheit*, CW 130, Dornach 1995, pp. 57ff; and Peter Selg, *Rudolf Steiner and Christian Rosenkreutz,* Steiner Books 2012.

25   Rudolf Steiner, *Das esoterische Christentum und die geistige Füh-rung der Menschheit*, CW 130, pp. 8off. Cf. Peter Selg, *Vom Logos menschlicher Physis. Die Entfaltung einer anthroposophischen Humanphysiologie im Werk Rudolf Steiner*, vol. I. Dornach 2006, pp. 241ff.

26   Rudolf Steiner, *From Jesus to Christ*, CW 131; and Sergei O. Pro-kofieff, *Mystery of the Resurrection in the Light of Anthroposophy*, Temple Lodge 2010.

27   "To the members of the Theosophical Society (German Section) and their friends, in relation to the St. John's building in Munich. On behalf of the administrative council of the St. John's building association." October/November 1911, p. 7. In Alexander Stra-kosch, *Lebenswege mit Rudolf Steiner. Erinnerungen*. Dornach 1994, p. 512.

28   Rudolf Steiner, *The Fall of the Spirits of Darkness*, CW 177, Rudolf Steiner Press 2008. Lectures of October 20 and 26, 1917.

29   Sergei O. Prokofieff, *Die erste Klasse der Michael-Schule und ihre christologischen Grundlagen*. Dornach 2009, p. 84.

30   It was in precisely this sense that Rudolf Steiner also described the work and mission of the School for Spiritual Science after it was "refounded" at the Christmas Foundation Meeting. "Our task today," said Steiner on December 29, 1923, with specific reference to the Michael age beginning in 1879, "is to receive and hold the full stream of spiritual life which, we can say, is coming toward us from the heights. In various places I have frequently told you that the first intimations of this new spiritual life was able to begin at the end of the 1870s, and then increased ever more as the cen-tury ended." *Die Weltgeschichte in anthroposophischer Beleuch-tung und als Grundlage der Erkenntnis des Menschengeistes*. CW 233, Dornach 1991, p. 113.) On January 23, 1923, eleven months before the beginning of the Christmas Foundation Meeting, in a lecture on the destruction by fire of the Goetheanum building, Steiner had said in Stuttgart: "The building in Dornach immeasur-ably increased the possibility of speaking of the spirituality neces-sary to humanity today. Through the Goetheanum, secrets of the world of spirit could indeed be communicated to a hugely increased number of people—through its visible forms and the visible work—than had ever previously been possible through the word. And first and foremost, those who had even the slightest modicum of good will to look with an open mind at the Goetheanum in Dor-nach, were able to see that it, and the Anthroposophy underlying it, were intrinsically non-sectarian; that Anthroposophy seeks to

encompass the great mission of our age, which is to enable human-kind to receive and hold the rays of a new spiritual light that have now become accessible to them and to infuse these into the instruments of human culture and civilization." (*Anthroposophische Gemeinschaftsbildung.* CW 257, Dornach 1989, p. 10.)

31 Cf. Peter Selg, *Rudolf Steiner (1861–1925). Lebens- und Werkgeschichte.* Vol. 1, pp. 678ff.

32 Rudolf Steiner, *Wie erlangt man Erkenntnisse der höheren Welten?* CW 10, Dornach 1993, p. 214.

33 Rudolf Steiner and Marie Steiner von Sivers, *Briefwechsel und Dokumente 1901–1925.* CW 262. Dornach 2002, p. 59.

34 Compare this wording with the process of reenlivening of "dead thoughts"—in so far as these are *"useful"*—by the beings of the angeloi, as Steiner described it in lesson 17 of the First Class. In *Esoterische Unterweisungen für die erste Klasse der Freien Hochschule für Geisteswissenschaft am Goetheanum 1924.* CW 270b. Dornach 2008, p. 137.

35 Rudolf Steiner, *Das esoterische Christentum und die geistige Führung der Menscheit.* CW 130, pp. 80ff.

36 See Rudolf Steiner, *Bilder okkulter Siegel und Säulen. Der Münchener Kongress Pfingsten 1907 und seine Auswirkungen.* CW 284. Dornach 1993, pp. 154ff.

37 For more on the details of this general assembly, and what occurred there, see Uwe Werner, "Ereignischronik 'Gesellschaft für theosophische Art und Kunst' 1911–1947" in Robin Schmidt (ed.), *Gesellschaft für theosophische Art und Kunst—1911. Dokumente und Interpretationen zur Geschichte und Gegenwart eines Impulses.* Dornach 2012, pp. 28ff; and Peter Selg, "Christian Rosenkreutz, die Stiftung der 'Gesellschaft für theosophische Art und Kunst' und der 'Kalender 1912/13'" in Rudolf Steiner, *Seelenkalender. In der Fassung der Handschrift.* Ed. Peter Selg, Arlesheim 2012, pp. 66ff.

38 Rudolf Steiner, *Zur Geschichte und aus den Inhalten der ersten Abteilung der Esoterischen Schule 1904–1914.* CW 264. Dornach 1996, pp. 427ff.

39 Peter Selg, *Rudolf Steiner und Christian Rosenkreutz*, pp. 38ff.

40 Cf. Sergei O. Prokofieff, *Die Erste Klasse der Michael-Schule und ihre christologischen Grundlagen*, pp. 20ff.

41 Cf. Sergei O. Prokofieff, *Die Geburt der christlichen Esoterik im 20. Jahrhundert und die ihr widerstrebenden Mächte.* Dornach 1997, pp. 23 ff.

42 Rudolf Steiner, *Zur Geschichte und aus den Inhalten der ersten Abteilung der Esoterischen Schule 1904–1914*. CW 264, p. 435.

43 Rudolf Steiner, *Der Goetheanumgedanke inmitten der Kulturkrisis der Gegenwart. Gesammelte Aufsätze aus der Wochenschrift "Das Goetheanum" 1921–1925*. CW 36. Dornach 1961, p. 39.

44 Rudolf Steiner, *Inneres Wesen des Menschen und Leben zwischen Tod und neuer Geburt*. CW 153. Dornach 1997, p. 14.

45 Cf. Peter Selg, *Christian Morgenstern. Sein Weg mit Rudolf Steiner*. Stuttgart 2014, pp. 244ff; and Peter Selg, *Geistige Hilfeleistung. Rudolf Steiner und Christian Morgenstern*. Arlesheim 2014, pp. 46ff.

46 Cf. Peter Selg, *Rudolf Steiner (1861–1925). Lebens- und Werkgeschichte*. Vol. 2, pp. 1540ff.

47 Rudolf Steiner, *Die Wirklichkeit der höheren Welten. Einführung in die Anthroposophie*. CW 79. Dornach 1988, p. 173. Author's emphases.

48 Rudolf Steiner, *Das Schicksalsjahr 1923 in der Geschichte der Anthroposophischen Gesellschaft. Vom Goetheanumbrand zur Weihnachtstagung*. CW 259. Dornach 1991, p. 254.

49 Rudolf Steiner, *Introducing Anthroposophical Medicine,* CW 312. Anthroposophic Press 1999. (The German title, *Geisteswissenschaft und Medizin*, did not originate with Steiner. The course was originally advertised under the title "Spiritual-scientific professional course for physicians and medical students"; for more on the circumstances that gave rise to the course, and the context in which it was held, cf. Peter Selg, *Dr. Oskar Schmiedel. 1887–1959. Der erste anthroposophische Pharmazeut und Weleda-Direktor.* Arlesheim 2010, pp. 68ff.)

50 Cf. Rudolf Steiner, *Das Schicksalsjahr 1923 in der Geschichte der Anthroposophischen Gesellschaft. Vom Goetheanumbrand zur Weihnachtstagung*. CW 259. Dornach 1991, pp. 251 f., 353 f.

51 Rudolf Steiner, *Der Goetheanumgedanke inmitten der Kulturkrisis der Gegenwart. Gesammelte Aufsätze aus der Wochenschrift "Das Goetheanum" 1921–1925*. CW 36. Dornach 1961, p. 328.

52 According to Marie Savitch Rudolf Steiner rejected use of the term "opening" in regard to the Goetheanum before the opening events began, "He stressed…in particular that this event was in no way to be seen as an opening of the Goetheanum, nor should this word be used for it. It would not be an opening. (*Marie Steiner-von Sivers. Mitarbeiterin Rudolf Steiners*. Dornach 1965, p. 114.) In a review of the events that he later wrote, Steiner said that he was against "celebrating a festive opening of the Goetheanum when the

first event was held there," and went on: "The program of lectures given there could not be seen as the occasion for such a celebration. This could only happen once it had become possible to hold an event whose whole tenor would have been in full accord with the original idea of the building." (*Der Goetheanum-Bau inmitten der Kulturkrisis der Gegenwart.* CW 36, pp. 329f.) According to Marie Savitch, in 1922 already Steiner planned to hold a festive inauguration of the Goetheanum at Christmas 1923/24, including the performance of a fifth Mystery play (*Marie Steiner-von Sivers. Mitarbeiterin Rudolf Steiners.* Dornach 1965, p. 130).

53 Cf. Peter Selg, *Rudolf Steiner (1861–1925). Lebens- und Werkgeschichte.* Vol. 2, pp. 1620ff.

54 Rudolf Steiner, *Esoterische Unterweisungen für die erste Klasse der Freien Hochschule für Geisteswissenschaft am Goetheanum 1924.* CW 270a, p. 150.

55 Rudolf Steiner. *Die Konstitution der Allgemeinen anthroposophischen Gesellschaft und der Freien Hochschule für Geisteswissenschaft. Der Wiederaufbau des Goetheanum.* CW 260a, p. 172.

56 Rudolf Steiner, *Esoterische Unterweisungen für die erste Klasse der Freien Hochschule für Geisteswissenschaft am Goetheanum 1924.* CW 270c, p. 191.

57 Rudolf Steiner, *Die Konstitution der Allgemeinen Anthroposophischen Gesellschaft und der Freien Hochschule für Geisteswissenschaft. Der Wiederaufbau des Goetheanum.* CW 260a, p. 172.

58 Rudolf Steiner, *Esoterische Unterweisungen für die erste Klasse der Freien Hochschule für Geisteswissenschaft am Goetheanum 1924.* CW 270c, p. 191.

59 Ibid., p. 12.

60 Rudolf Steiner, *Die Weihnachtstagung zur Begründung der Allgemeinen Anthroposophischen Gesellschaft 1923/24.* CW 260. Dornach 1994, p. 79.

61 Cf. Rudolf Steiner, *Das Schicksalsjahr 1923 in der Geschichte der Anthroposophischen Gesellschaft. Vom Goetheanumbrand zur Weihnachtstagung.* CW 259; Peter Selg, "Das Schicksalsjahr 1923—Rudolf Steiner's Weg zur Weihnachtstagung, in Sergei O. Prokofieff/Peter Selg, *Die Weihnachtstagung und die Begründung der Neuen Myterien.* Arlesheim 2011, pp. 11–38; Peter Selg, *Die Identität der Allgemeinen Anthroposophischen Gesellschaft.* Arlesheim 2012, pp. 15–40; and Peter Selg, *Rudolf Steiner (1861–1925). Lebens- und Werkgeschichte.* Vol. 3, pp. 1651–1801.

62 Rudolf Steiner, *Esoterische Unterweisungen für die erste Klasse der Freien Hochschule für Geisteswissenschaft am Goetheanum 1924*. CW 270c, p. 191.

63 Rudolf Steiner, *Die Konstitution der Allgemeinen Anthroposophischen Gesellschaft und der Freien Hochschule für Geisteswissenschaft. Der Wiederaufbau des Goetheanum (1924–1925)*. CW 260a, p. 190.

64 Rudolf Steiner, *Esoterische Unterweisungen für die erste Klasse der Freien Hochschule für Geisteswissenschaft am Goetheanum 1924*. CW 270c, p. 14.

65 Rudolf Steiner, *Die Weihnachtstagung zur Begründung der Allgemeinen Anthroposophischen Gesellschaft 1923/24*. CW 260. p. 271.

66 Ibid., p. 94.

67 Ibid., p. 276.

68 Rudolf Steiner, *Die Konstitution der Allgemeinen Anthroposophischen Gesellschaft und der Freien Hochschule für Geisteswissenschaft. Der Wiederaufbau des Goetheanum (1924–1925)*. CW 260a, p. 100. In the "First Class" of the Goetheanum's esoteric school, stressed Steiner, the "practice of perception and knowledge" should be taught. The lessons should convey a "picture" of the experiences connected with actual penetration into the world of spirit; at the same time they should facilitate a reflective "after-experience" of, and sympathy with, corresponding experiences in the spirit—an "ideal reflection" drawing on elements of Imagination, Inspiration and Intuition. In the newsletter of the weekly periodical *Das Goetheanum*, Steiner wrote as follows by way of information for all members: "The 'School' will conduct the participant into realms of the world of spirit that cannot be revealed in the form of ideas. Here it becomes necessary to find means of expression for Imaginations, Inspirations and Intuitions" (Ibid., p. 109). "It is in fact the case that the esoteric deepening of which you can read so much in my book *How to Know Higher Worlds*, and about which I have also spoken so much, should arise henceforth through the three classes [of the School]" (Ibid., p. 124). Sergei O. Prokofieff indicated that Steiner began the first Class lesson at the point where the book *How to Know Higher Worlds* had ended—the encounter with the Guardian of the Threshold (cf. Sergei O. Prokofieff, *Die Erste Klasse der Michael-Schule und ihre christologischen Grundlagen*, p. 39).

69 Rudolf Steiner, *Die Konstitution der Allgemeinen Anthroposophischen Gesellschaft und der Freien Hochschule für*

Geisteswissenschaft. Der Wiederaufbau des Goetheanum (1924–1925). CW 260a, p. 358.

70   Ibid., p. 101.

71   Rudolf Steiner, *Die Weihnachtstagung zur Begründung der Allgemeinen Anthroposophischen Gesellschaft 1923/24.* CW 260. p. 142.

72   Cf. *Beiträge zur Rudolf Steiner Gesamtausgabe.* No. 105, Michaelmas 1990, pp. 37–38.

73   Rudolf Steiner, *Esoterische Unterweisungen für die erste Klasse der Freien Hochschule für Geisteswissenschaft am Goetheanum 1924.* CW 270a, p. 128.

74   Ibid., p. 129.

75   On February 6 1924, Steiner said in Stuttgart, "This Christmas Foundation Meeting has shown that, if the Anthroposophical Society is to continue to act in an effective way in future, it must depart from the ways it has pursued over the past ten years. It must reach inward from the society's external, outward forms into the inner spirit. It must in general acquire an esoteric character. What exists in future as the School for Spiritual Science in Dornach must bear a kind of esoteric character, as must the institution of the Society as a whole; and in so far as it does, the Society will be able to sustain the spiritual life which it needs. It must not externalize itself, as it has been at risk of doing over the past ten years." (*Die Konstitution der Allgemeinen Anthroposophischen Gesellschaft und der Freien Hochschule für Geisteswissenschaft. Der Wiederaufbau des Goetheanum (1924–1925).* CW 260a, p. 175).

76   Rudolf Steiner, *Esoterische Unterweisungen für die erste Klasse der Freien Hochschule für Geisteswissenschaft am Goetheanum 1924.* CW 270c, p. 125.

77   Ibid.

78   Rudolf Steiner, *Esoterische Unterweisungen für die erste Klasse der Freien Hochschule für Geisteswissenschaft am Goetheanum 1924.* CW 270a, p. 129.

79   Ibid., p. 124.

80   Rudolf Steiner, *Esoterische Unterweisungen für die erste Klasse der Freien Hochschule für Geisteswissenschaft am Goetheanum 1924.* CW 270c, p. 123.

81   Ibid.

82   Rudolf Steiner, *Esoterische Unterweisungen für die erste Klasse der Freien Hochschule für Geisteswissenschaft am Goetheanum 1924.* CW 270a, p. 149.

83 Rudolf Steiner, *Esoterische Unterweisungen für die erste Klasse der Freien Hochschule für Geisteswissenschaft am Goetheanum 1924*. CW 270c, p. 174.

84 Rudolf Steiner, *Esoterische Unterweisungen für die erste Klasse der Freien Hochschule für Geisteswissenschaft am Goetheanum 1924*. CW 270a, p. 149.

85 Ibid., p. 81.

86 Ibid., p. 1.

87 Ibid., p. 129.

88 Rudolf Steiner, *Esoterische Unterweisungen für die erste Klasse der Freien Hochschule für Geisteswissenschaft am Goetheanum 1924*. CW 270c, p. 114.

89 Ibid., p. 123.

90 In Thomas Meyer, *Ludwig Polzer-Hoditz. Ein Europäer*. Basel 2008, p. 669.

91 Rudolf Steiner, *Esoterische Unterweisungen für die erste Klasse der Freien Hochschule für Geisteswissenschaft am Goetheanum 1924*. CW 270b, p. 174.

92 Rudolf Steiner, *Esoterische Betrachtungen karmischer Zusammenhänge*. Vol. 4. CW 238. Dornach 1991, p. 72.

93 Cf. Peter Selg, "Krise und Neubeginn der Anthroposophischen Gesellschaft 1923/24," in, *Die Identität der Allgemeinen Anthroposophischen Gesellschaft*, pp. 13–52.

94 Numerous instances of this can be found in my documentation, *Rudolf Steiner. Life and Work*. Cf. also the enlarging study by Sergei O. Prokofieff, "Der manichäische Impuls im Leben Rudolf Steiners," in *Die okkulte Bedeutung des Verzeihens*. Stuttgart 1992, pp. 161ff.

95 See Peter Selg, *Rudolf Steiner (1861–1925). Lebens- und Werkgeschichte*. Vol. 3, pp. 1853ff. in relation to Rudolf Steiner's intention with the Leading Thoughts, and their inner connection with the impulses of the Christmas Foundation Meeting.

96 Rudolf Steiner, *Esoterische Betrachtungen karmischer Zusammenhänge*. Vol. 3. CW 237. Dornach 1991, p. 117.

97 Rudolf Steiner, *World History in the Light of Anthroposophy*, CW 233, Steiner Press 1977; and Peter Selg, "Rudolf Steiners Abendvorträge der Weihnachtstagung," in, Peter Selg and Marc Desaules (eds.), *Die Sozialgestalt der Weihnachtstagung*, pp. 89ff.

98 Rudolf Steiner, *Esoterische Betrachtungen karmischer Zusammenhänge*. Vol. 6. CW 240. Dornach 1992, p. 168.

99 See note 97.

100 Sergei O. Prokofieff, *Die Erste Klasse der Michael-Schule und ihre christologischen Grundlagen*, p. 83.

101 Rudolf Steiner, *Anthroposophische Leitsätze. Der Erkenntnisweg der Anthroposophie—Das Michael-Mysterium*. CW 26, p. 88.

102 For more on these sacrifices, see Rudolf Steiner, *Approaching the Mystery of Golgotha*, CW 152, and Peter Selg, *Die Leiden der nathanischen Seele. Anthroposophische Christologie am Vorabend der Ersten Weltkriegs*. Arlesheim 2014 (shortly to be published in English by AP). In relation to Michael's involvement in these processes, see Sergei O. Prokofieff, *Der Jahreskreislauf als Einweihungsweg zum Erleben der Christus-Wesenheit*. Stuttgart 1996, pp. 35ff.

103 Rudolf Steiner, *Esoterische Betrachtungen karmischer Zusammenhänge*. Vol. 6. CW 240. Dornach, p. 167.

104 The Mystery of Golgotha began already with the departure of the Christ from the Sun sphere and his turning toward the Earth. "In his lecture in Torquay on August 21, 1924, Steiner emphasized that Michael and his hosts saw Christ 'leaving the Sun at the time of the Mystery of Golgotha.' Since, in his lectures on the 'Fifth Gospel,' Steiner described how the Christ (sun) spirit only entirely or fully incarnated into the body of Jesus at Golgotha at the moment he died, this was very probably the culmination of the 'departure' from the Sun." (Peter Selg, *Grundstein der Zukunft. Vom Schicksal der Michael-Gemeinschaft*. Arlesheim 2013, p. 82.)

105 Cf. Rudolf Steiner, "Was ist die Erde in Wirklichkeit im Makrokosmos?" in, *Anthroposophische Leitsätze. Der Erkenntnisweg der Anthroposophie—Das Michael-Mysterium*. CW 26, pp. 197–201.

106 Rudolf Steiner, *Esoterische Betrachtungen karmischer Zusammenhänge*. Vol. 6. CW 240. Dornach, p. 169.

107 Cf. in particular Rudolf Steiner's lectures on 7.13.1924 (Dornach, CW 237), 7.18.1924 (Arnheim, CW 240), 8.14.1924 (Torquay, CW 243) and 9.12.1924 (Dornach, CW 238).

108 Rudolf Steiner, *Esoterische Betrachtungen karmischer Zusammenhänge*. Vol. 3. CW 237. Dornach 1991, p. 111.

109 Rudolf Steiner, *Anthroposophische Leitsätze. Der Erkenntnisweg der Anthroposophie—Das Michael-Mysterium*. CW 26, p. 62.

110 Cf. Rudolf Steiner, *Anthroposophie und Rosenkreuzertum. Ausgewählte Texte*. Ed. Andreas Neider. Dornach 2007; and Peter Selg, *Rudolf Steiner und Christian Rosenkreutz*.

111 Rudolf Steiner, *Esoterische Betrachtungen karmischer Zusammenhänge*. Vol. 3. CW 237. Dornach 1991, p. 112.

112 Ibid., p. 123.

113   Sergei O. Prokofieff, *Das Michael-Mysterium. Eine geisteswis-senschaftliche Betrachtung der Michael-Imagination und ihrer Darstellung in Eurythmie.* Arlesheim 2014, p. 99. See pages 93–99 in relation to the whole scope of the teachings of the suprasensory Michael School.

114   Rudolf Steiner, *Esoterische Betrachtungen karmischer Zusammenhänge.* Vol. 3. CW 237. Dornach 1991, p. 113.

115   Rudolf Steiner, *Das Prinzip der spirituellen Ökonomie im Zusammenhang mit Wiederverkörperungsfragen.* CW 109. Dornach 2000, p. 157. Cf. also Peter Selg, *Rudolf Steiner und Christian Rosenkreutz,* pp. 38ff.

116   Rudolf Steiner, *Esoterische Betrachtungen karmischer Zusammenhänge.* Vol. 4. CW 238, p. 70.

117   Rudolf Steiner, *Esoterische Betrachtungen karmischer Zusammenhänge.* Vol. 3. CW 237, p. 115.

118   Ibid., p. 116.

119   Cf. Peter Selg, *Vom Logos menschlicher Physis. Die Entfaltung einer anthroposophischen Humanphysiologie im Werk Rudolf Steiners.* Vol. 2, Dornach 2006, pp. 519ff and pp. 634 ff.

120   Rudolf Steiner, *Esoterische Betrachtungen karmischer Zusammenhänge.* Vol. 6. CW 240. p. 190.

121   Rudolf Steiner, *Esoterische Betrachtungen karmischer Zusammenhänge.* Vol. 3. CW 237, p. 114.

122   Ibid.

123   "Someone who really feels drawn toward Anthroposophy, feels an urge for it, today has in his soul the after-effects arising from his former absorption, in the circles around Michael, of the heavenly Anthroposophy which preceded Anthroposophy on Earth. The teaching at that time given by Michael prepared what was to become Anthroposophy on Earth" (Ibid., p. 117).

124   Thomas Meyer, "Die übersinnliche Michaelschule," in *Der Meditationsweg der Michaelschule in neunzehn Stunden. Rudolf Steiners esoterisches Vermächtnis aus dem Jahre 1924,* ed. Thomas Meyer, Basel 2011, p. 433.

125   Cf. Rudolf Steiner, *Mysterienstätten des Mittelalters. Rosenkreuzertum und modernes Einweihungsprinzip. Das Osterfest als ein Stück Mysteriengeschichte der Menschheit.* CW 233a, lecture of 1.6.1924.

126   Cf. Rudolf Steiner, "Esoteric Christianity and the Spiritual Guidance of Humanity," CW 130, lecture of 12.18.1912 (and subsequent accounts).

127   See also note 219.

128 Rudolf Steiner, *Esoterische Betrachtungen karmischer Zusammenhänge*. Vol. 4. CW 238, p. 92.

129 Ibid.

130 Rudolf Steiner, *Esoterische Betrachtungen karmischer Zusammenhänge*. Vol. 6. CW 240. p. 179. Author's emphasis.

131 Cf. the lecture in London on May 2, 1913, in *Approaching the Mystery of Golgotha*, CW 152; and Peter Selg, *Die Leiden der nathanischen Seele. Anthroposophische Christologie am Vorabend des Ersten Weltkriegs* [In English: *The Sufferings of the Nathan Soul: Anthroposophic Christology on the Eve of World War I*, SteinerBooks 2016], pp. 74ff.

132 Sergei O. Prokofieff, *Das Michael-Mysterium. Eine geisteswissenschaftliche Betrachtung der Michael-Imagination und ihrer Darstellung in Eurythmie*, p. 102. Author's emphasis.

133 Ibid.

134 "If we have the ability to recognize souls in their bodies, we will perceive those who worked with us in the first half of the 19th century, when mighty cosmic Imaginations were invoked in the suprasensory world which represent what I would call the new Christianity. Then—as now in bodies on Earth—souls were gathered in order to create reality from what I will call the cosmic substantiality and cosmic forces, whose mighty pictures had cosmic significance and were the prelude to what should be accomplished on Earth as anthroposophic teaching and actions. I would put it like this: The very greatest majority of anthroposophists who meet and sit together could, if they recognized this, be aware that they know each other, were together in the world of spirit, and, in a suprasensory cultus, shared mighty cosmic Imaginations together!" Rudolf Steiner, *Esoterische Betrachtungen karmischer Zusammenhänge*. Vol. 6. CW 240. p. 146.

135 Cf. Peter Selg, *Das Wesen und die Zukunft der Anthroposophischen Gesellschaft*, Arlesheim 2013, pp. 14ff.

136 Cf. Peter Selg, "'Es walten die Übel...' Die Grundsteinlegung vom 20. September 1913" in, *Grundstein zur Zukunft. Vom Schicksal der Michael-Gemeinschaft*. Arlesheim 2013, pp. 11ff.

137 Ibid.

138 Cf. Rudolf Steiner, *Aus den Inhalten der esoterischen Stunden*, vol. III: 1913 and 1914; 1920–1923. CW 266c, Dornach 1998, p. 499. Steiner used this verse at the beginning of almost all the esoteric lessons which he gave in the postwar years up to the new founding of the esoteric school as "School for Spiritual Science." He later returned to it in the sequence of lessons of the First Class.

139   Rudolf Steiner, *Die Weihnachtstagung zur Begründung der Allge-
       meinen Anthroposophischen Gesellschaft 1923/24*. CW 260, p.
       270. Author's emphasis.

140   Rudolf Steiner, *Esoterische Betrachtungen karmischer Zusam-
       menhänge*. Vol. 6. CW 240. p. 185.

141   Rudolf Steiner, *Aus den Inhalten der esoterischen Stunden*. CW
       266a. Dornach 2007, p. 262.

142   "I admit that I keep having to ask myself now whether I should or I
       should not. But it seems to me that nothing will be gained by speak-
       ing of these things only in the abstract. And so all caution must
       be set aside in order to speak of specific things and instances. The
       world must take things as it sees fit. Inner spiritual necessities exist
       for the spread of Anthroposophy. One takes one's lead from what is,
       as it were, kindled in one by spiritual necessities, rather than pursu-
       ing any kind of outward-oriented "opportunity." Opportunism has
       already done enough harm to the Anthroposophical Society, and
       should no longer be practiced in future. And even if some things
       seem very paradoxical indeed, yet one should still simply express
       them in future" (Rudolf Steiner, *Esoterische Betrachtungen kar-
       mischer Zusammenhänge*. Vol. 6. CW 240. pp. 180f).

143   Rudolf Steiner, *Esoterische Betrachtungen karmischer Zusam-
       menhänge*. Vol. 6. CW 240, p. 157.

144   Despite very limited uptake of the impulse of the Christmas Foun-
       dation Meeting, Rudolf Steiner still spoke of this future prospect
       in his last address on September 20, 1924. After far-reaching com-
       ments on the individuality of Novalis, who, in his short life (1772–
       1801) had become active on Earth as a "messenger" of the Michael
       stream, Steiner said, "And so we see in Novalis, specifically, an
       illustrious herald of that Michael stream, my dear friends, which
       should now lead and guide you all while you live; and then, once
       you have passed through the gate of death, you will find all those
       souls—including the being I have spoken of—in the suprasensory,
       spiritual world, all those with whom you should prepare the work
       that should be done at the end of this century to lead humanity
       through and beyond the great crisis it is encountering" (Rudolf
       Steiner, *Esoterische Betrachtungen karmischer Zusammenhänge*.
       Vol 4. CW 238, pp. 172f).

145   Cf. Sergei O. Prokofieff, *Das Rätsel des menschlichen Ich. Eine
       anthroposophische Betrachtung*. Dornach 2013; and Sergei O. Pro-
       kofieff, *Die Erste Klasse der Michael-Schule und ihre Christolo-
       gischen Grundlagen*, pp. 69–163.

146 Cf. Sergei O. Prokofieff, *Der esoterische Weg durch die neunzehn Klassenstunden im Lichte des übersinnlichen Mysteriums von Golgotha and des Fünften Evangelium.* Dornach 2014, pp. 25–58 (for School members).

147 Rudolf Steiner, *Esoterische Unterweisungen für die erste Klasse der Freien Hochschule für Geisteswissenschaft am Goetheanum 1924.* CW 270a, p. 151.

148 Rudolf Steiner, *Die Weihnachtstagung zur Begründung der Allgemeinen Anthroposophischen Gesellschaft 1923/24.* CW 260, p. 280.

149 Peter Selg, *Rudolf Steiner (1861–1925). Lebens- und Werkgeschichte.* Vol. 3, pp. 1958ff.

150 Sergei O. Prokofieff, *Die Erste Klasse der Michael-Schule und ihre christologischen Grundlagen,* p. 116.

151 Rudolf Steiner, *Esoterische Unterweisungen für die erste Klasse der Freien Hochschule für Geisteswissenschaft am Goetheanum 1924.* CW 270b, p. 90.

152 Cf. Peter Selg, "Die Anthroposophie und das menschliche Herz," in *Michael und Christus. Studien zur Anthroposophie Rudolf Steiner.* Arlesheim 2010, pp. 73–109.

153 Rudolf Steiner, *Esoterische Unterweisungen für die erste Klasse der Freien Hochschule für Geisteswissenschaft am Goetheanum 1924.* CW 270b, p. 174.

154 Rudolf Steiner, *Esoterische Unterweisungen für die erste Klasse der Freien Hochschule für Geisteswissenschaft am Goetheanum 1924.* CW 270c, p. 14.

155 Ibid., p. 126.

156 Cf. Sergei O. Prokofieff, *Die Begegnung mit dem Bösen und seine Überwindung in der Geisteswissenschaft.* Dornach 1999; and "Das Weltenschicksal des Bösen" in *Und die Sonne wird zur Erde. Zum Mysterium der Auferstehung,* Arlesheim 2012, pp. 287–393.

157 Rudolf Steiner, *Anthroposophische Leitsätze. Der Erkenntnisweg der Anthroposophie—Das Michael-Mysterium.* CW 26, p. 92.

158 Rudolf Steiner, *Esoterische Betrachtungen karmischer Zusammenhänge.* Vol. 3. CW 237, p. 134.

159 This suggests that in November 1924 Rudolf Steiner by no means considered the "First Class" to have been "fully established." A widespread interpretation holds that the First Class was completed with the nineteenth Class lesson, and that Rudolf Steiner's announcement of the subsequent second and third part or "stage" (cf. p. [60]) should be identified as the Second and Third Class of the esoteric school. Thomas Meyer and others however, have raised

the fact that on August 2 1924 Steiner did not announce the end of the "First Class" but only of its first "stage," and offered the prospect of continuation of the teaching content of the *First Class* "in a second and even a third stage" (see Thomas Meyer, "Die irdische Michaelschule" in *Der Meditationsweg der Michaelschule in neunzehn Stunden. Rudolf Steiners esoterisches Vermächtnis aus dem Jahre 1924*, p. 440). By contrast, Johannes Kiersch writes, "This raises the question...as to whether the quoted formulation during the nineteenth lesson...might not allow a different interpretation. Could it not be the case that Steiner was referring to the first stage of the School "in the form of this First Class"? Hella Wiesberger points to a note by Marie Steiner in March 1926, where she writes, "He left us before he could bring the work he had begun to completion, before he was able to give us what he called the Second and Third Class. In the Second Class he wished to give us the cultus that would have corresponded to revelations, flowing out into Imaginations, of the suprasensory school of Michael at the [end of the 18th and beginning of the] 19th century."

Marie Steiner seems here to consider it self-evident that the continuation of the Class lessons announced for September are not a second stage of the First Class, but would have been a Second Class, and that therefore the contents of the First Class can be regarded as complete." (Johannes Kiersch, *Steiners individualisierte Esoterik einst und jetzt. Zur Entwicklung der Freien Hochschule für Geisteswissenschaft*, p. 62.) Ita Wegman also clearly understood Steiner's comments in the nineteenth Class lesson, on 8.2.1924, as an announcement of the Second and Third Class. On August 16 1925 she wrote in the newsletter, "Shortly before his illness, Dr. Steiner had already decided to establish the Second and Third Class." (In *Was in der Anthroposophischen Gesellschaft vorgeht. Nachrichten für deren Mitglieder.* Year 2, no. 33, p. 129.)

It is hard to discuss this complex matter since there is no firm knowledge about what Steiner exactly envisaged (apart from his brief indication on 8.2.1924) and everything else is speculative. It seems to me that the views of Marie Steiner-von Sivers and Ita Wegman have weight not only because they were both close to Rudolf Steiner but also because responsibility for the course of nineteen lessons would have placed an unwavering requirement on every colleague of Steiner's in whose hands they were placed. Furthermore we should consider that the continuation announced by Steiner on August 2, 1924 was *inwardly* compatible with statements made to Polzer about the emphasis and aims of (as well as the people involved in) the Second and Third Class (see below). It remains unclear however—as does much else—what Steiner meant when he said that the First Class still needed to become "fully established" despite the fact that the nineteen lessons had been completed.

160 In Thomas Meyer, *Ludwig Polzer-Hoditz. Ein Europäer*, pp. 665f. As regards the authenticity of these discussion notes, that are not extant in Polzer-Hoditz's handwriting, see ibid pp. 671ff. According to Emil Leinhas, Polzer-Hoditz wrote down Rudolf Steiner's comments of 11.11.1924 directly after his visit in the studio (*Einige Gesichtspunkte zum Verständnis der Vorgänge in der Anthroposophischen Gesellschaft und Bewegung nach Rudolf Steiner's Tod— Ein Versuch*. Stuttgart 1963, p. 53).

161 "Frau Dr. Steiner told Roman Boos that Dr. Steiner had wished to entrust the Second Class to her, with only 36 members. He himself would have retained leadership of the Third Class, with a still smaller number." (Letter from Hilde Boos-Hamburger to Emil Leinhas, 7.23.1963. Documentation at the Goetheanum, quoted in Thomas Meyer, *Der Meditationsweg der Michaelschule in neunzehn Stunden. Rudolf Steiners esoterisches Vermächtnis des Jahres 1924*. Supplementary volume, p. 249.).

162 Sergei O. Prokofieff, *Das Michael-Mysterium. Eine geisteswissenschaftliche Betrachtung der Michael-Imagination und ihrer Darstellung in Eurythmie*, p. 162.

163 Rudolf Steiner, *Wahrspruchworte*. CW 40. Dornach 2005, p. 93.

164 Quoted in Johannes Kiersch, *Zur Entwicklung der Freien Hochschule für Geisteswissenschaft. Die Erste Klasse,* p. 274.

165 Cf. J. Emanuel Zeylmans van Emmichoven, *Who Was Ita Wegman. A Documentation*. Vol. 1, Mercury Press 1995.

166 Rudolf Steiner, *Die Weihnachtstagung zur Begründung der Allgemeinen Anthroposophischen Gesellschaft 1923/24*. CW 260, p. 57.

167 Ita Wegman, draft for a lecture in London, 2.27.1933. Typescript. Ita Wegman Archive. Cf. Emanuel Zeylmans van Emmichoven, *Wer war Ita Wegman. Eine Dokumentation*. Vol. I, p. 294.

168 Ibid.

169 Rudolf Steiner, *Esoterische Betrachtungen karmischer Zusammenhänge*. Vol. 3. CW 237, p. 92. For inner connections between the Michael cultus and the images of Goethe's fairytale, see Sergei O. Prokofieff, *Das Michael-Mysterium. Eine geisteswissenschaftliche Betrachtung der Michael-Imagination und ihrer Darstellung in Eurythmie*, pp. 101ff.

170   Ita Wegman, draft for a lecture in London, 2.27.1933. Typescript.
      Ita Wegman Archive. Cf. Emanuel Zeylmans van Emmichoven,
      Wer war Ita Wegman. Eine Dokumentation. Vol. I, p. 294.

171   Ibid.

172   In relation to the spiritual background to the separation of the
      esoteric schools, cf. for instance Hilla Wiesberger, *Rudolf Steiner
      esoterische Lehrtätigkeit. Wahrhaftigkeit, Kontinuität, Neugestal-
      tung.* Dornach 1997, pp. 133ff.; Sergei O. Prokofieff, *Die Geburt
      der christlichen Esoterik im 20. Jahrhundert und die ihr wider-
      strebenden Mächte.* Dornach 1997, pp. 23ff.; and Thomas Meyer,
      "Der christologische Grundirrtum der Theosophen" in, *Scheidung
      der Geister. Die Bodhisattvafrage als Prüfstein des Unterscheid-
      ungsvermögens.* Basel 2010, pp. 33ff.

173   Cf. Peter Selg, *"Ich bleibe bei Ihnen." Rudolf Steiner und Ita Weg-
      man. München, Pfingsten 1907. Dornach 1923–1925.* Stuttgart
      2007, pp. 39ff.

174   Ita Wegman Archive, Arlesheim. First published in J. Emanuel Zey-
      lmans van Emmichoven, *Wer war Ita Wegman. Eine Dokumenta-
      tion.* Vol. I, pp. 206ff.

175   Ita Wegman, draft for a lecture in London, 2.27.1933. Typescript.
      Ita Wegman Archive. Cf. J. Emanuel Zeylmans van Emmichoven,
      Wer war Ita Wegman. Eine Dokumentation. Vol. I, p. 295; and
      Peter Selg, *"Ich bleibe bei Ihnen." Rudolf Steiner und Ita Wegman.
      München, Pfingsten 1907. Dornach 1923–1925.* Stuttgart 2007,
      pp. 43f.

176   Rudolf Steiner, *Aus den Inhalten der esoterischen Stunden.* CW
      266a, p. 251.

177   Peter Selg, *"Ich bleibe bei Ihnen." Rudolf Steiner und Ita Wegman.
      München, Pfingsten 1907. Dornach 1923–1925.* Stuttgart 2007,
      pp. 76ff.

178   Ita Wegman, draft for a lecture in London, 2.27.1933. Typescript.
      Ita Wegman Archive. Cf. J. Emanuel Zeylmans van Emmichoven,
      Wer war Ita Wegman. Eine Dokumentation. Vol. I, p. 296; and
      Peter Selg, *"Ich bleibe bei Ihnen." Rudolf Steiner und Ita Wegman.
      München, Pfingsten 1907. Dornach 1923–1925.* Stuttgart 2007, p.
      44.

179   Rudolf Steiner, *Die Anthroposophie und ihre Gegner 1919–1921.*
      CW 255b. Dornach 2003, p. 335.

180   Ita Wegman Archive, Arlesheim. Facsimile and transcript in J.
      Emanuel Zeylmans van Emmichoven, *Wer war Ita Wegman. Eine
      Dokumentation.* Vol. I, pp. 290f.

181 Cf. however the isolated esoteric lessons between 1920–1923 in Rudolf Steiner, *Aus den Inhalten der esoterischen Stunden*. (Vol. III, 1913 and 1914; 1920–1923), CW 266c, pp. 351ff. In a faculty meeting of teachers in Stuttgart at the end of 1921, when Steiner was asked about the possibility of continuing the esoteric lessons of the prewar period, he spoke of esotericism as a "painful chapter of the anthroposophic movement": "I had to leave this to one side because esotericism was misused in the most shameful way" (*Konferenzen mit den Lehrern der Freien Waldorfschule 1921–1923*. CW 300b, Dornach 1975, pp. 58f). But far more than a "painful chapter" in the anthroposophic movement as such, it was one as regards the Anthroposophical *Society*—and after 1918 Rudolf Steiner was also willing to cultivate the development of limited, task-related esoteric *communities* within the anthroposophic movement, as can be seen, among other things, from the history of the "esoteric youth group" (from October 1922 onward) as well as the development of the movement for religious renewal or the "Young Doctors" movement. All these began their work prior to the Christmas Foundation Meeting, with Rudolf Steiner's great attentiveness and support.

182 Ita Wegman, notebooks, around 1927 (words of farewell to medical students at the end of a course). Ita Wegman Archive, Arlesheim. Cf. also J. Emanuel Zeylmans van Emmichoven, *Wer war Ita Wegman. Eine Dokumentation*. Vol. I, p. 310.

183 Cf. Rudolf Steiner, *Die Weltgeschichte in anthroposophischer Beleuchtung und als Grundlage der Erkenntnis des Menschengeistes*. CW 233; and Peter Selg, "Rudolf Steiners Abendvorträge der Weihnachtstagung," in Peter Selg and March Desaules (eds.), *Die Sozialgestalt der Weihnachtstagung*, pp. 91ff.

184 "To my dear Mysa—January 13, 1924 Rudolf Steiner." Ita Wegman Archive, Arlesheim. In J. Emanuel Zeylmans van Emmichoven, *Die Erkraftung des Herzens. Eine Mysterienschulung für die Gegenwart. Rudolf Steiners Zusammenarbeit mit Ita Wegman*. Arlesheim 2009, p. 230.

185 Cf. Peter Selg, *Rudolf Steiner (1861–1925). Lebens- und Werkgeschichte*. Vol. 3, pp. 1711ff.

186 Rudolf Steiner, *Das Schicksalsjahr 1923 in der Geschichte der Anthroposophischen Gesellschaft. Vom Goetheanumbrand zur Weihnachtstagung*. CW 259, p. 302.

187 Rudolf Steiner, letter to Edith Maryon, 3.25.1923, in *Rudolf Steiner / Edith Maryon, Briefwechsel. Briefe—Sprüche—Skizzen, 1912 –1924*. CW 263a. Dornach 1990, p. 117.

188 For more on the historical context of this question, cf. Peter Selg, *"Ich bleibe bei Ihnen." Rudolf Steiner und Ita Wegman. München, Pfingsten 1907.* Dornach, 1923–1925, pp. 56ff.

189 Cf. Sergei O. Prokofieff, *Menschen mögen es hören. Das Mysterium der Weihnachtstagung.* Stuttgart 2002, pp. 392f. in relation to questions about Marie von Sivers and Ita Wegman and their importance for the anthroposophic movement.

190 Count Ludwig Polzer-Hoditz, address at the annual meeting of the Anthroposophical Society on April 14, 1935 in Dornach. Printed in, J. Emanuel Zeylmans van Emmichoven, *Wer war Ita Wegman. Eine Dokumentation.* Vol. 3, Heidelberg 1992, p. 335.

191 J. Emanuel Zeylmans van Emmichoven, *Die Erkraftung des Herzens. Eine Mysterienschulung der Gegenwart. Rudolf Steiners Zusammenarbeit mit Ita Wegman,* pp. 127ff.

192 Rudolf Steiner, letter to Ita Wegman, 6.10.1924. Ita Wegman Archive, Arlesheim. First published in J. Emanuel Zeylmans van Emmichoven, *Wer war Ita Wegman. Eine Dokumentation.* Vol. I, pp. 206ff.

193 Ita Wegman Archive. In, J. Emanuel Zeylmans van Emmichoven, *Die Erkraftung des Herzens. Eine Mysterienschulung der Gegenwart. Rudolf Steiners Zusammenarbeit mit Ita Wegman,* pp. 139ff.

194 Rudolf Steiner, letter to Ita Wegman, 6.10.1924. Ita Wegman Archive, Arlesheim. First published in J. Emanuel Zeylmans van Emmichoven, *Wer war Ita Wegman. Eine Dokumentation.* Vol. I, pp. 206ff.

195 Rudolf Steiner, *Okkulte Geschichte. Esoterische Betrachtungen karmischer Zusammenhänge von Persönlichkeiten und Ereignissen der Weltgeschichte.* CW 126, Dornach 1992, p. 18.

196 Count Ludwig Polzer-Hoditz, address at the annual meeting of the General Anthroposophical Society on April 14, 1935 in Dornach. Printed in, J. Emanuel Zeylmans van Emmichoven, *Wer war Ita Wegman. Eine Dokumentation.* Vol. 3, p. 335.

197 Ita Wegman Archive, Arlesheim. In J. Emanuel Zeylmans van Emmichoven, *Die Erkraftung des Herzens. Eine Mysterienschulung der Gegenwart. Rudolf Steiners Zusammenarbeit mit Ita Wegman,* pp. 404ff.

198 Ita Wegman, letter to Maria Roeschl, 2.22.1935. Ita Wegman Archive, Arlesheim. In Peter Self, *Geistiger Widerstand und Überwindung. Ita Wegman 1933–1935,* Dornach 2005, pp. 199ff.

199 Rudolf Steiner, *Esoterische Unterweisungen für die erste Klasse der Freien Hochschule für Geisteswissenschaft am Goetheanum 1924.* CW 270c, p. 15.

200 Rudolf Steiner, *Anthroposophische Menschenerkenntnis und Med-izin*. CW 319, Dornach 1994, p. 220.

201 Cf. the lectures of 8.14 and 21.1924 in Rudolf Steiner, *Das Initi-aten-Bewusstsein. Die wahren und die falschen Wege der geistigen Forschung*. CW 243; and J. Emanuel Zeylmans van Emmichoven, *Wer war Ita Wegman. Eine Dokumentation*. Vol. 2, pp. 109ff.

202 In relation to these processes and their importance for understanding Steiner's concept of the School, see my monographs, *Helene von Grunelius und Rudolf Steiners Kurse für junge Mediziner. Eine biographische Studie.* Dornach 2003; *Die Briefkorrespon-denmz der "jungen Mediziner." Eine dokumentarische Studie zur Rezeption von Rudolf Steiners "Jungmediziner"-Kursen.* Dornach 2005; *Die "Wärme-Meditation." Geschichtlicher Hintergrund und ideelle Beziehungen.* Dornach 2005; *"Die Medizin muss Ernst machen mit dem gieistigen Leben." Rudolf Steiners Hochschul-kurse für die "jungen Mediziner."* Dornach 2006.

203 Rudolf Steiner, *Meditative Betrachtungen und Anleitungen zur Vertiefung der Heilkunst. Vorträge für Ärzte und Medizinstudier-ende.* CW 316, Dornach 2009, p. 110.

204 Ibid., p. 137; author's emphasis.

205 In relation to Rudolf Steiner's clinical collaboration with Ita Weg-man, culminating among other things in shared development of the medical textbook *Extending the Art of Medicine*, see for example my monograph, *"Und in der Tat, dies wirkte." Die Kran-kengschichten des Buches "Grundlegendes für eine Erweiterung der Heilkunst nach geisteswissenschaftlichen Erkenntnissen" von Rudolf Steiner und Ita Wegman. Eine Dokumentation.* Dornach 2007. Even prior to its publication, Rudolf Steiner stressed the relevance to the School at Dornach of the book cowritten with Ita Wegman: "Through the efforts of Frau Dr. Wegman and myself in Dornach, this character will enter medicine in a forthcoming publication which speaks frankly and freely of what occult knowledge can give to medicine. This was the deepest impulse underlying the Christmas Foundation Meeting..." (*Die Konstitution der Allge-meinen Anthroposophischen Gesellschaft und der Freien Hoch-schule für Geisteswissenschaft.* CW 260a, p. 489).

206 Rudolf Steiner, *Meditative Betrachtungen und Anleitungen zur Vertiefung der Heilkunst. Vorträge für Ärzte und Medizinstudier-ende.* CW 316, p. 220.

207 In relation to Steiner's development work in the various School sections, see Peter Selg, *Rudolf Steiner (1861–1925). Lebens- und Werkgeschichte.* Vol. 3, pp. 1878–1922.

208 Ita Wegman, notebook entry, undated (1935). Ita Wegman Archive, Arlesheim. Facsimile reproduced in Peter Selg, *Geistiger Widerstand und Überwindung. Ita Wegman 1933–1935*, p. 176.

209 Ita Wegman, letter to Albert Steffen, 3.16.1926. Ita Wegman Archive, Arlesheim. First published in J. Emanuel Zeylmans van Emmichoven, *Wer war Ita Wegman. Eine Dokumentation.* Vol. 3, pp. 65ff.

210 For more on the way in which applications for admission to the School were personally dealt with by Rudolf Steiner, see the detailed archive study by Kurt Franz David, *Die Einrichtung der Ersten Klasse durch Rudolf Steiner und deren Schicksale bis zur Gegenwart,* photocopied manuscript, Documentation at the Goetheanum 1974, pp. 30–34. (Passages from this work are quoted in Peter Selg, *Rudolf Steiner und die Freie Hochschule für Geisteswissenschaft. Die Begründung der Ersten Klasse*, pp. 150ff.) Cf. also Sergei O. Prokofieff/Peter Selg, *Die Weihnachtstagung und die Begründung der Neuen Mysterien,* Arlesheim 2011, pp. 93–102. According to testimony from Ita Wegman, even before September 1924 Rudolf Steiner conducted admission conversations in her presence, though without using ritual elements ("Don't forget that I was always present at the admissions, at these conversations, from the beginning right up to the end, not only here in Dornach but also abroad," she wrote on 3.16.1926 to Albert Steffen. "Previously [before September 1924] the admissions took place in my presence without my direct participation, and without the festive character of the handshake" (Ita Wegman Archive, Arlesheim).

211 Wolfgang Moldenhauer, letter to Kurt Franz David, 11.15.1972. Quoted in Johannes Kiersch, *Zur Entwicklung der Freien Hochschule für Geisteswissenschaft. Die Erste Klasse.* Dornach 2005, p. 51.

212 Cf. Rudolf Steiner, *Esoterische Unterweisungen für die erste Klasse der Freien Hochschule für Geisteswissenschaft am Goetheanum 1924,* CW 270c, pp. 30, 45, 63, 82, 102, 122, 127, 219.

213 Ita Wegman, draft for a lecture in London, 2.27.1933. Typescript. Ita Wegman Archive, Arlesheim. Cf. also J. Emanuel Zeylmans van Emmichoven, *Wer war Ita Wegman. Eine Dokumentation,* vol. I, p. 315.

214 Cf. Rudolf Steiner, *Esoterische Unterweisungen für die erste Klasse der Freien Hochschule für Geisteswissenschaft am Goetheanum 1924,* CW 270b, p. 176.

215 Quoted in Irene Diet, *Jules und Alice Sauerwein und der Kampf um die Anthroposophie in Frankreich.* Zeist 1998, p. 200.

216 Friedrich Rittelmeyer, *Meine Lebensbegegnung mit Rudolf Steiner*, Stuttgart 1983, pp. 156f.

217 Cf. Rudolf Steiner, *Esoterische Unterweisungen für die erste Klasse der Freien Hochschule für Geisteswissenschaft am Goetheanum 1924.* CW 270c, p. 218.

218 Rudolf Steiner, *Esoterische Unterweisungen für die erste Klasse der Freien Hochschule für Geisteswissenschaft am Goetheanum 1924,* CW 270c, p. 218.

219 Ibid., p. 219. For the possible background to introduction of the cultic seals and signs of Michael at the end of August 1924 in London, cf. the comments by Thomas Meyer, "Neunzehn Ausschlüsse und ein Verrat in England" in, *Der Meditationsweg der Michaelschule in neunzehn Stunden. Rudolf Steiners esoterisches Vermächtnis des Jahres 1924.* Supplementary volume, pp. 242f. There, with reference to statements by Madeleine van Deventer and Erich Kirchner, Thomas Meyer suggests that the cultic or ritual elements had been introduced to the Class after a "betrayal" of the mantras by an Englishman, which Steiner had learned of between the two lessons in London on August 25 and 27, 1924. In this context Thomas Meyer also refers to Steiner's London karma lecture on August 27, where he spoke among other things of the materialistic (and fundamentally anti-Aristotelian) impulses of Francis Bacon. Bacon, who died at Highgate near London on April 9, 1626, during the Thirty Years' War, brought demonic powers ("idols") with him into the after-death world. The individualities of Aristotle and Alexander, in their membership of the Michael community, battled against these forces. The soul of Alexander did so in particular. Nevertheless they continued to be active as "inspirers of materialism in the nineteenth century," as Steiner described on August 27, 1924, and they continue to work to this day. Thomas Meyer writes, "The betrayal [of the mantras] in London appears like...a *reflection* of the spiritual conflict in the suprasensory Michael School, albeit one with very real potency, which now threatened to penetrate into the Michael School that *had been fetched down to Earth.* Introduction of the sign and seal of Michael served to ward off this battle. The betrayal in England, the introduction of these 'defensive' or protective measures, and Steiner's comments in the lecture in London that we have quoted, all belong together. In the light of this whole picture we can also directly understand why Ita Wegman was now assigned a new role in the continuing lessons. This new role was nothing other than the earthly continuation of her suprasensory activity in battling with the Baconian idols" (Ibid., p. 245).

220 Rudolf Steiner, *Esoterische Unterweisungen für die erste Klasse der Freien Hochschule für Geisteswissenschaft am Goetheanum 1924*, CW 270c, p. 214.

221 Ibid., p. 14.

222 Ibid., pp. 9/89/111.

223 Minutes of a meeting of the executive council at the Goetheanum [Vorstand] with the general secretaries and delegates of the General Anthroposophical Society. Dornach, 4.25.1930. Documentation at the Goetheanum.

224 Cf. Peter Selg, "'Benedictus deus qui dedit nobis signum.' Das Aufnahmeritual in die Leitung der Michael-Schule." In, *Rudolf Steiner und Christian Rosenkreutz*, pp. 111–126. Corrected reprint in the appendix of this book, pp. 105ff.

225 Rudolf Steiner, *Esoterische Unterweisungen für die die erste Klasse der Freien Hochschule für Geisteswissenschaft am Goetheanum 1924*. CW 270c, p. 28.

226 Cf. Sergei O. Prokofieff, *Die Erste Klasse der Michael-Schule und ihre christologischen Grundlagen*, pp. 69–163.

227 Cf. Peter Selg, *Rudolf Steiner und Christian Rosenkreutz*, pp. 13ff.

228 See appendix, pp. [109f].

229 Ita Wegman Archive, Arlesheim. In J. Emanuel Zeylmans van Emmichoven, *Die Erkraftung des Herzens. Eine Mysterienschulung der Gegenwart. Rudolf Steiners Zusammenarbeit mit Ita Wegman,* p. 357.

230 Ita Wegman, "An die Mitglieder!" in *Was in der Anthroposophischen Gesellschaft vorgeht. Nachrichten für deren Mitglieder.* 2nd year, no. 40, 10.4.1925, p. 153.

231 Cf. Peter Selg, *Rudolf Steiner (1861–1925). Lebens- und Werkgeschichte,* vol. III, pp. 2012–2113.

232 Ita Wegman, draft for a lecture in London, 2.27.1933. Typescript. Ita Wegman Archive. Cf. also J. Emanuel Zeylmans van Emmichoven, *Wer war Ita Wegman. Eine Dokumentation*, vol. I, p. 316.

233 Notebook, undated (1924/25), Ita Wegman Archive, Arlesheim. In J. Emanuel Zeylmans van Emmichoven, *Wer war Ita Wegman. Eine Dokumentation.* Vol. I, p. 320.

234 Cf. Peter Selg, *Rudolf Steiner (1861–1925). Lebens- und Werkgeschichte.* Vol. 3, pp. 1955ff.

235 Ita Wegman Archive, Arlesheim. First published in J. Emanuel Zeylmans van Emmichoven, *Wer war Ita Wegman. Eine Dokumentation.* Vol. I, p. 316.

236 Ita Wegman Archive, Arlesheim. In J. Emanuel Zeylmans van Emmichoven, *Die Erkraftung des Herzens. Eine*

Mysterienschulung der Gegenwart. Rudolf Steiners Zusammenarbeit mit Ita Wegman, pp. 382ff. After Rudolf Steiner's death, Ita Wegman sought to awaken amongst members of the Anthroposophical Society at least an initial understanding of *this* dimension of Rudolf Steiner's battle after the Christmas Foundation Meeting. His efforts related also to the First Class and its importance for combating the powers of evil. Wegman spoke of the workings of demons in the first essay she wrote after Steiner's death about the last period of his life. She wrote it on Good Friday 1925, for members of the Anthroposophical Society, and sent it to Albert Steffen. But Steffen, as editor of the journal, did not print the relevant passage (cf. Ita Wegman's letter to Albert Steffen of 4.11.1925, in J. Emanuel Zeylmans van Emmichoven, *Wer war Ita Wegman. Eine Dokumentation*. Vol. 3, pp. 57ff).

At Michaelmas 1925, half a year after Rudolf Steiner's death, Ita Wegman made a further, more detailed attempt to write an account of this time, writing in an essay for the newsletter, "To the members!" the following among other things: "It is surely now time to speak about these things again, and it would be wrong to fail to pass on important things that our teacher said. We live in difficult times, and it is high time, surely, to gain insight into spiritual occurrences. Rudolf Steiner told me one day that anti-Michael demons are ruthlessly endeavoring to prevent Michael's work from thriving, and to destroy it. They conceal these intentions, and only human beings can draw the demons' secrets from them. Only human beings can have knowledge of demons' secrets. The gods are waiting for these secrets that humankind brings toward them; and it is the gods alone who in turn can decipher these demonic secrets to human beings. The dark deeds of these demons can be averted when human beings wrest their secrets from them and offer them to the gods, so that, where darkness prevailed, spiritual light can once more shine forth. These anti-Michael demons, which include Klingsor and his hosts, were hard at work and made taunting threats to wreak havoc when the Michael impulses, so strongly instigated, were unable to make a breakthrough. My anxious question was this: What will happen if this does not succeed? And the answer I received: Then karma will take its course" (In *Was in der Anthroposophischen Gesellschaft vorgeht. Nachrichten für deren Mitglieder*. Year 2, no. 40, 10.4.1925, p. 153). In her text Ita Wegman was paraphrasing a mantra that she had received from Rudolf Steiner. Cf. J. Emanuel Zeylmans van Emmichoven, *Die Erkraftung des Herzens*, p.382ff.

237 Ita Wegmn Archive, Arlesheim. In J. Emanuel Zeylmans van Emmichoven, *Die Erkraftung des Herzens. Eine Mysterienschulung der Gegenwart. Rudolf Steiners Zusammenarbeit mit Ita Wegman*, pp. 254f.

238 "And as soon as daylight comes, let us continue the treatment that I suggested." (R. Steiner) in Ita Wegman, "Das Krankenlager, die letzen Tage und Stunden Dr. Steiners" in *Was in der Anthroposophischen Gesellschaft vorgeht. Nachrichten für deren Mitglieder.* Year 2, no. 16, 4.19.1925, p. 63. Reprinted in Ita Wegman, *Erinnerung an Rudolf Steiner,* ed. Peter Selg, Arlesheim 2011, p. 64. In relation to Rudolf Steiner's medical collaboration with Ita Wegman and his initiative for diagnosis and therapy, cf. also the documented case histories in my monograph, *"Und in der Tat, dies wirkte." Die Krankengeschichten des Buches "Grundlegendes für eine Erweiterung der Heilkunst nach geisteswissenschaftlichen Erkenntnissen" von Rudolf Steiner und Ita Wegman.* Dornach 2007.

239 Cf. among other things Rudolf Steiner's communications to members in the period of his illness, in which he repeatedly said how grateful he was for Wegman's therapeutic efforts and support (*Die Konstitution der Allgemeinen Anthroposophischen Gesellschaft und der Freien Hochschule für Geisteswissenschaft. Der Wiederaufbau8 des Goetheanum (1924–1925).* CW 260a, pp. 400–404). See also his last mantric transcripts for her, which he gave her at Christmas 1924: "In the star script of the universe / Can be read what unites us / In the star script / That reveals itself / In the heart's depths. // In the love script of the soul / Lives the faithful sacrifice of the heart / That you bring me daily / Love script will become / Star script in the heights of the universe. // At Christmastide / The soul feels deeply / What lives within; / The love-stars'-script of gratitude / Inwardly I offer you" (Ita Wegman Archive, Arlesheim. In J. Emanuel Zeylmans van Emmichoven, *Die Erkraftung des Herzens. Eine Mysterienschulung der Gegenwart. Rudolf Steiners Zusammenarbeit mit Ita Wegman,* pp. 398ff).

240 Ita Wegman, draft for a lecture in London, 2.27.1933. Typescript. Ita Wegman Archive, Arlesheim. First published in J. Emanuel Zeylmans van Emmichoven, *Wer war Ita Wegman. Eine Dokumentation. Vol.* I, p. 316.

241 Steffen not only noted Ita Wegman's "failure" but in this context also his own interpretation of the period of Rudolf Steiner's illness. This was to have serious consequences in the further destiny of the general Anthroposophical Society and the Goetheanum, playing in to the "Memorandum" published in 1935, and

contributing to Wegman's expulsion from the Society: "I leave with a terrible sense of anxiety. Yes, she is to blame. Outwardly she cared for him, but inwardly she held him captive. She kept at bay all who could be there for him by finding the enthusiasm for deeds and works. But she can do nothing and knows nothing. She pushed herself between him and others." Archive of the Albert Steffen Foundation. First published in Johannes Kiersch, *Steiners individualisierte Esoterik einst und jetzt. Zur Entwicklung der Freien Hochschule für Geisteswissenschaft*, p. 247. For a more realistic account of Steiner's illness from October 1924 to the end of March 1925, and of Ita Wegman's efforts during this period, see Peter Selg, *Rudolf Steiner (1861–1925). Lebens- und Werkgeschichte*. Vol. 3, pp. 1958ff.

242 Cf. Peter Selg, *Albert Steffen. Begegnung mit Rudolf Steiner.* Dornach 2009, pp. 154ff.

243 This was still how Erdmuth Johannes Grosse mistakenly interpreted her words in 2006: "This conversation was a kind of confession that she wished to…make to him" (*Das Rätsel des Urvorstandes. Blicke auf die Konflikte in der Anthroposophischen Gesellschaft nach Rudolf Steiners Tod. Eine karmisch–psychologische Betrachtung.* Dornach 2006, p. 118).

244 Ibid., p. 58.

245 Documentation at the Goetheanum.

246 "*Good Friday, 7 p.m.*: a reading of the new tragedy 'Hieram and Solomon' by Albert Steffen. *Easter Sunday 7 p.m.*: Eurythmy performances. *Easter Monday 8 p.m.*: Lecture by Albert Steffen" (In *Was in der Anthroposophischen Gesellschaft vorgeht. Nachrichten für deren Mitglieder.* Year 2, no. 15, p. 60).

247 Cf. J. Emanuel Zeylmans van Emmichoven, *Wer war Ita Wegman. Eine Dokumentation.* Vol. 3. *Kämpfe und Konflikte 1924 bis 1935*, p. 57.

248 Ibid., p. 58.

249 In relation to this core mission of the General Anthroposophical Society and the Goetheanum as School for Spiritual Science, of internalizing the insights of anthroposophic spiritual science in tangible and detailed ways, and publicly demonstrating their topicality and relevance in the face of threats to civilization, cf. among other things Rudolf Steiner's comments on the Christmas Foundation Meeting and his innovative esssay "To the Members!" of 7.6.1924. In, *Die Konstitution der Allgemeinen Anthroposophischen Gesellschaft und der Freien Hochschule für Geisteswissenschaft. Der Wiederaufbau des Goetheanum.* CW 260a, pp. 77ff. Cf. also Peter

Selg, *Rudolf Steiner (1861–1925). Lebens- und Werkgeschichte.*
Vol. 3, pp. 1853–1859.

250   Ibid., pp. 1971ff.

251   Cf. J. Emanuel Zeylmans van Emmichoven, *Wer war Ita Wegman.*
Eine Dokumentation. Vol. 3. *Kämpfe und Konflikte 1924 bis 1935.*

252   When Ita Wegman held her first Class lesson in Dornach on June
4, 1925, she was led in by Albert Steffen who introduced her as the
"secretary" entrusted with this role by the executive council, a
formulation which, according to Elisabeth Vreede, ran *counter* to
previous agreements according to which his introduction should
have expressed Ita Wegman's special responsibility for the First
Class. In 1935, Vreede described these events in her memoirs ("On
the History of the Anthroposophical Society Since the Christmas
Foundation Meeting") and added this commentary: "This was
like a slap in the face for me, for this wording entirely concealed
the fact of Fr. Dr. W.'s special connection with the Class, and presented her as someone who had been in some way "commissioned"
by the executive council without revealing why she in particular had been assigned this task" (In Peter Selg, *Elisabeth Vreede.*
1879–1943, p. 142).

A year and a half after the Class lesson in question, Albert Steffen wrote in a letter to Friedrich Rittelmeyer: "In my statement to
the gathering of Class members I expressly used the word "secretary," and this was taken down in the shorthand transcript. Later,
too, I maintained this view" (Dec. 7, 1926. Dokumentation am
Goetheanum. Quoted in Johannes Kiersch, *Steiners individualisert*
Esoterik einst und jetzt. Zur Entwicklung der freien Hochschule
für Geisteswissenschaft, p. 107). Steffen's introductory words were
first made public in the study by Kiersch. They are not entirely
unambiguous in relation to Ita Wegman, and at the end refer to
"our highly esteemed friend" (Ibid., p. 264). But Steffen's diary
entries on the previous day (June 3, 1925) display his pronounced
ambivalence, his doubts, and his antipathy toward her. Johannes
Kiersch likewise published these diary comments, which include
the following: "I am filled with dejection. I wish I could avoid the
event tomorrow. Do I trust Frau Dr. Wegman? Is she worthy of
this? The very fact that I ask this suggests otherwise. But she is
closest to Dr. Steiner. He speaks through her. She has the task of
passing on the verses" (ibid). In relation to accusations developing
in Dornach in the following months, and intensifying up to the
expulsions in 1935, that, based on karmic pretensions, Wegman
had "arrogantly" secured a special position in relation to the First

Class, and de facto sought to take over its leadership (and thus leadership of the whole School for Spiritual Science), see the testimonies compiled in J. Emanuel Zeylmans van Emmichoven, *Who Was Ita Wegman. A Documentation.* Vol. 3.

253   Ibid. In his 2005 publication *Zur Entwicklung der Freien Hochschule für Geisteswissenschaft. Die Erste Klasse* (new, expanded edition 2012), Johannes Kiersch was the first to document in detail the Class-related occurrences and discussions after Mar. 30, 1925. Here he showed also that individual, highly gifted anthroposophists such as Eugen Kolisko and Walter Johannes Stein, who had understoiod Rudolf Steiner's karma lectures in their relation to the history and destiny of the Anthroposophical Society, emphatically urged Marie Steiner-von Sivers and Albert Steffen to acknowledge Ita Wegman. Their insistance, however, only further intensified the existing antipathy toward—and real fear of—her, and hugely exacerbated the situation. But, in my view, to classify people such as Walter Johannes Stein and Eugen Kolisko as (only) "over-zealous devotees" of Ita Wegman (*Steiners individualisierte Esoterik einst und jetzt. Zur Entwicklung der Freien Hochschule für Geisteswissenschaft,* p. 78) ignores the reality of their differentiated relationship with Wegman and their spiritual independence (cf. the collected correspondence of Eugen Kolisko and Walter Johannes Stein with Ita Wegman in the Ita Wegman Archive, Arlesheim). To do full justice to them and their supposed "zealousness," it would instead be helpful to try to put oneself in their situation at the time. It had become clear to them, with striking existential vividness, what and who Steiner had been speaking about in the evening lectures of the Christmas Foundation Meeting and in the karma lectures (cf. Peter Selg, "Eugen Kolisko." In *Anfänge anthroposophischer Heilkunst.* Dornach 2000, pp. 160ff.). At the same time they were disconcerted to see that leading individuals in Dornach, who would be instrumental in the Society's ongoing destiny, had no awareness of this (or were actively suppressing and thus dismissing it). In this situation their vehemence was anything other than well judged, yet we should recognize that Kolisko and Stein themselves were not the problem, but were attempting, for their part, to respond to a situation of grave difficulty.

254   "A list held in the London archive of the Anthroposophical Society in Great Britain refers to 35 [Class] Lessons [held by Ita Wegman] up to Nov. 22, 1931" (Johannes Kiersch, *Steiners individualisierte Esoterik einst und jetzt. Zur Entwicklung der freien Hochschule für Geisteswissenschaft,* p. 110).

255 Ita Wegman, "An die Mitglieder!" In, *Was in der Anthroposophischen Gesellschaft vorgeht. Nachrichten für deren Mitglieder.* Year 2, no. 35, Aug. 16, 1925, p. 129. In 1924, Rudolf Steiner held twelve Class lessons outside Dornach: in Prague (Apr. 3, 5), Bern (Apr. 17), Paris (May 26, 27), Breslau (June 12, 13), Arnheim (July 22, 23), Torquay (Aug. 19) and London (Aug. 25, 27).

256 Ita Wegman, "An die Mitglieder!" In, *Was in der Anthroposophischen Gesellschaft vorgeht. Nachrichten für deren Mitglieder.* Year 2, no. 24, June 14, 1925, p. 96.

257 In relation to the spiritual organism of the nineteen lessons cf. the studies by Sergei O. Prokofieff, *Die Erste Klasse der Michael-Schule und ihre christologischen Grundlagen* (Dornach 2009) and *Der esoterische Weg durch die neunzehn Klassenstunden im Lichte des übersinnlichen Mysteriums von Golgotha und des Fünften Evangelium* (Dornach 2014).

258 Rudolf Steiner, *Aus der Akasha-Forschung. Das Fünfte Evangelium.* CW 148. Dornach 1992, p. 324.

259 Cf. Sergei O. Prokofieff, *Der esoterische Weg durch die neunzehn Klassenstunden im Lichte des übersinnlichen Mysteriums von Golgotha und des Fünften Evangelium.*

260 Ita Wegman, letter to Albert Steffen, March 16, 1926. Ita Wegman Archive, Arlesheim. The letter is reprinted in Rudolf Steiner, *Esoterische Unterweisungen für die erste Klasse der Freien Hochschule für Geisteswissenschaft am Goetheanum 1924.* CW 270a, pp. 198f.

261 Peter Selg, *Rudolf Steiner und die freie Hochschule für Geisteswissenschaft. Die Begründung der "Ersten Klasse,"* pp. 92f. These words were taken from conversations with Marianne Fiechter-Bischof (Apr. 3, 1915–Sep. 30, 2014) who attended all the Class lessons given by Wegman in Arlesheim between August 1937 and December 1942. See also the notebooks of Marianne Fiechter-Bischof in the Ita Wegman Archive, Arlesheim.

262 Johannes Kiersch, after viewing all available documents, also acknowledged in his study that Ita Wegman had never undertaken any discernible attempt to position herself as "sole leader of the School," but had, rather, hoped for many years that the esoteric executive council might develop unity and unanimity. "Nor did she ever make reference to the intimate conversations she had with Rudolf Steiner about their shared karma. It was quite alien to her to use such things to assert claims to power" (*Steiners individualisierte Esoterik einst und jetzt. Zur Entwicklung der Freien Hochschule für Geisteswissenschaft,* p. 95). On the other hand, in Nov.

2012, in the Dornach weekly periodical *Das Goetheanum* and thus fully and influentially in the public domain, Kiersch wrote as follows about Wegman's inner situation in 1925, in an essay on the First Class (in the section entitled "Ita Wegman's knowledge and destiny"): "Under the impression of intimate communications in Penmaenmawr and everything that followed from this, she identified herself with the person of the Sun hero Alexander of Macedonia, as described by her spiritual teacher in the karma lectures of the previous summer [1924]." No doubt Wegman was not "clear," he goes on, "how strictly Rudolf Steiner had warned against citing the accomplishments of a former life in relation to work in a present one" (Das Goetheanum, no. 47, Nov. 24, 2012, p. 11).

263 Ita Wegman, "An die Mitglieder!" In, *Was in der Anthroposophischen Gesellschaft vorgeht. Nachrichten für deren Mitglieder.* Year 2, no. 24, Apr. 14, 1925, p. 96.

264 Ita Wegman, draft for introductory words for a Class lesson in Vienna (1925). Ita Wegman Archive, Arlesheim. In Peter Selg, *Rudolf Steiner und die Freie Hochschule für Geisteswissenschaft. Die Begründung der "Ersten Klasse."* Arlesheim 2008, pp. 112f. (facsimile and transcription). Here Wegman likewise referred to the context in which her responsibility for the Class was first established, formulating this as follows (in her account in the newsletter of June 14, 1925, see above): "When Rudolf Steiner established this Michael School, an institution, as he said, that was inaugurated by the world of spirit, he designated me his colleague in this School. Therefore, my dear friends, after the death of our teacher I did not feel myself to be released from my obligations to the Michael School, but on the contrary I feel more connected with them than ever. I had to give serious weight to Dr. Steiner's words about the Michael School as an institution of the world of spirit, since I regard the world of spirit, and the laws streaming forth from it, as realities."

265 Cf. Sergei O. Prokofieff, *Die Erste Klasse der Michaelschule und ihre christologischen Grundlagen* und *Der esoterische Weg durch die neunzehn Klassenstunden im Lichte des übersinnlichen Mysteriums von Golgotha und des Fünften Evangelium.*

266 Rudolf Steiner, *Esoterische Unterweisungen für die erste Klasse der Freien Hochschule für Geisteswissenschaft am Goetheanum 1924.* CW 270c, p. 123.

267 Ibid.

268 For more about the spiritual conception of this concept of leadership, see, for example, Peter Selg, *Der Vorstand, die Sektionen*

und die Gesellschaft. Welche Hochschule wollte Rudolf Steiner? Arlesheim 2011.

269 Cf. Peter Selg, *Rudolf Steiner (1861–1925). Lebens- und Werkgeschichte*. Vol. 3, pp. 2027f.

270 Cf. Peter Selg, *Rudolf Steiner und Christian Rosenkreutz*, pp. 49ff.

271 Cf. in this context J. Emanuel Zeylmans van Emmichoven, *Wer war Ita Wegman. Eine Dokumentation*. Vol. 3. *Kämpfe und Konflikte 1924 bis 1935*, pp. 70–77. Johannes Kiersch writes about Ita Wegman's "apparently almost naïve blindness for certain social situations," citing among things the reaction to Wegman's essays: "With her letters 'To the members!' she causes considerable discomfort in the Anthroposophical Society, which she is unable to remedy later with her efforts at self-justification, however persuasive these might be in themselves. Above all, however, many members feel irritated by the grandiose scope of her reflections" (*Steiners individualiserte Esoterik einst und jetzt. Zur Entwicklung der Freien Hochschule für Geisteswissenschaft*, pp. 86f.).) And yet a good deal more than a few members of the General Anthroposophical Society were extremely grateful for Ita Wegman's essays, which she had to stop publishing due to the criticism in Dornach. In her literary estate (Ita Wegman Archive, Arlesheim) there are are over 200 letters (signed by over 440 people) from individuals, 23 branches, 26 working groups, the faculty of the Waldorf School in Stuttgart and a national society (Belgium) thanking her warmly for her initiative in furthering the intentions of the Christmas Foundation Meeting. These people were by no means all "zealous devotees" of Ita Wegman, not did they all (or even the majority) belong to her medical-therapeutic movement or even her "karmic stream."

272 Rudolf Steiner, *Esoterische Unterweisungen für die erste Klasse der Freien Hochschule für Geisteswissenschaft am Goetheanum 1924*. CW 270c, p. 63.

273 Ibid., p. 14; author's emphasis.

274 Rudolf Steiner, *Die Weihnachtstagung zur Begründung der Allgemeinen Anthroposophischen Gesellschaft 1923/24*, p. 35.

275 Cf. Peter Selg, "Der Weg zu Christus—die Verwandlung des menschlichen Bewusstseins," in, *Anthroposophie weltweit*. Special issue, November 2014, p. 6 (in relation to Sergei O. Prokofieff, *Der esoterische Weg durch die neunzehn Klassenstunden im Lichte des übersinnlichen Mysteriums von Golgotha und des Fünften Evangelium*. Dornach 2014.

276 Sergei O. Prokofieff, *Die Erste Klasse der Michael-Schule und ihre christologischen Grundlagen*, p. 147.

277 Rudolf Steiner, *Wie erlangt man Erkenntnisse der höheren Welten?* CW 10, p. 149.

278 *Esoterische Unterweisungen für die erste Klasse der Freien Hochschule für Geisteswissenschaft am Goetheanum 1924*. CW 270c, p. 161.

279 Cf. Peter Selg, *Die Leiden der nathanischen Seele. Anthroposophische Christologie am Vorabend des Ersten Weltkriegs*, pp. 74 ff.

280 For more on this dismal theme and the contemporary debate, many years *prior* to the start of the first "euthanasia" measures in Nazi Germany, cf. among other sources the detailed documentation by the medical historian Udo Benzenhöfer, *Der gute Tod? Geschichte der Euthanasie und Sterbehilfe*. Göttingen 2009, pp. 81–96.

281 Ita Wegman Archive, Arlesheim.

282 In relation to the situation when this verse was given, cf. Anna Samweber, "Aus meinem Leben. Erinnerungen an Rudolf Steiner und Marie Steiner-von Sivers," in Peter Selg, *Michael als Genius der Zivilisationsentwicklung. Rudolf Steiners Abschied von Berlin. Potsdamer Strasse 39a, 23. Mai 1923*. Arlesheim 2013, pp. 50f.

283 Johannes Kiersch, *Zur Entwicklung der Freien Hochschule für Geiseswissenschaft. Die Erste Klasse*. Dornach 2005, p. 83. (Unaltered also in Johannes Kiersch, *Steiners individualisierte Esoterik einst und jetzt. Zur Entwicklung der Freien Hochschule für Geisteswissenschaft*. Dornach 2012, p. 105.)

284 Ibid., p. 111.

285 Rudolf Steiner, *Esoterische Unterweisungen für die erste Klasse der Freien Hochschule für Geisteswissenschaft am Goetheanum 1924*. CW 270a, p. 128.

286 Cf. Peter Selg, *Geistiger Widerstand und Überwindung. Ita Wegman 1933–1935*, pp. 13ff.

287 Cf. J. Emanuel Zeylmans van Emmichoven, *Wer war Ita Wegman. Eine Dokumentation*. Vol. 3; and Peter Selg, *Geistiger Widerstand und Überwindung. Ita Wegman 1933–1935* [in English: *Spiritual Resistance: Ita Wegman 1933–1935*. SteinerBooks 2015].

288 Rudolf Steiner, *Esoterische Unterweisungen für die erste Klasse der Freien Hochschule für Geisteswissenschaft am Goetheanum 1924*. CW 270c, p. 12.

289 Cf. Peter Selg, *Geistiger Widerstand und Überwindung. Ita Wegman 1933–1935*, pp. 155ff.

290 Ibid., pp. 162ff.

291 Ita Wegman, letter to Maria Röschl, Feb. 22, 1935. Ita Wegman Archive, Arlesheim.

292 Ita Wegman, letter to Alice Wengraf, Jan. 31, 1935. Ibid.

293   Quoted in Thomas Meyer, *Ludwig Polzer-Hoditz. Ein Europäer.*
       Basel 2008, pp. 669.

294   In Peter Selg, *Geistiger Widerstand und Überwindung. Ita Weg-
       man 1933–1935*, p. 163. According to information from the Son-
       nenhof, Werner Pache's original diary is no longer extant. Thomas
       Meyer transcribed passages from it many years ago in the course
       of his research, and made these available to Emanuel Zeylmans
       van Emmichoven (Ita Wegman Archive, Arlesheim). Johannes
       Kiersch interpeted the note quoted in my book *Geistiger Wider-
       stand und Überwindung* as the start of "free Class lessons." Ita
       Wegman, according to his comments, had "undergone a complete
       change in her inner stance toward her work as esoteric teacher,"
       "developing more innovative ideas," and ultimately passing from
       "guarding and preserving the words [of Rudolf Steiner] as these
       were passed down" to "free lessons" in the sense in which this is
       nowadays understood (*Zur Entwicklung der freien Hochschule.
       Die Erste Klasse,* pp. 172/83/177f).

       In my monograph *Rudolf Steiner und die Freie Hochschule für
       Geisteswissenschaft. Die Begründung der Ersten Klasse,* I showed
       that there were no historical records or contemporary reports sug-
       gesting that Ita Wegman had held "free Class lessons" (in this
       understanding of the phrase) but that, on the contrary, Dr. Mari-
       anne Fiechter-Bischof, who attended Class lessons held by Wegman
       up to December 1942 (cf. note 261) had described to me how, to the
       very end, Wegman adhered to the precise words and formulations
       of Rudolf Steiner, and that therefore in my view Pache's note must
       be understood in a quite different sense. In response to these find-
       ings, however, Johannes Kiersch made only very minor changes to
       the corresponding passages in the second edition of his study. He
       continued to assume that on Jan. 27, 1935, Wegman had held a
       "free lesson" in Arlesheim before a group specially organized with
       this in mind, writing among other things: "We cannot exclude the
       possibility that other gatherings, limited to this strictly confidential
       group of ten people, followed this 'beginning.'"

       Wegman may also have been compelled to observe, already at
       this meeting, that participants could not or did not wish to follow
       her, that the situation was not yet ready for what she had conceived"
       (*Steiners individualisierte Esoterik einst und jetzt*, p. 204). No one
       can completely exclude the possibility that what Kiersch imagines
       was so, even if this is speculative, and not historically documented.
       Neither Madeleine van Deventer nor Margarethe Kirchner-Bock-
       holt, nor other participants at the meeting on Jan. 27, 1935, ever

mentioned anything in this regard. Wegman frequently did surprising things, sometimes to the bafflement of those in her closer or broader surroundings. But it seems very improbable that she would have held a first "free Class lesson" after her grave illness, her profound experiences in Palestine and on Capri, her return to Arlesheim, and eight days after the death of her mother, which strongly affected her.

According to all notebook entries and the letters of previous months (large numbers of which can be found in her literary estate), the form of the Class lessons was not something she was giving any consideration to at this time. Of paramount concern to her, rather, was the question of separating Michaelic esotericism from the problems and ownership claims in Dornach, and indeed from the whole leadership group of the Anthroposophical Society as such. I have spoken in the foreword and text of my publication, referred to above, about the problematic nature of regarding, of all people, Ita Wegman as leader of a supposed movement opposed to "guarding and preserving the words [of Rudolf Steiner] as these were passed down" and to "backward-looking" orientation to "sacred traditions in the form of preserved texts." Everything that we know suggests that this was not how she regarded Anthroposophy; it was neither her stance nor her style. In relation to the Class, the Anthroposophical Society, the Goetheanum and Rudolf Steiner, Wegman has been the subject of more than enough speculations and conjectures already, and indeed has repeatedly been the object and victim of the most varied insinuations about things that had little to do with her. It therefore seems to me wise to be wary of overly hasty interpretations.

295   Ita Wegman, letter to Gertrud Goyert, 1.29.1935. Ita Wegman Archive, Arlesheim.

296   Cf. Peter Selg, *Die letzten drei Jahre. Ita Wegman in Ascona 1940–1943*, Dornach 2006, pp. 122ff; and Sergei O. Prokofieff, *Occult Significance of Forgiveness*, Steiner Press 2004. Cf. also my summarizing study "Über Ita Wegman und die Anthroposophische Gesellschaft," in, *Initiative Entwicklungsrichtung Anthroposophie. Ein Nachrichtenblatt* no. 8, 2013, pp. 1–4.

297   Rudolf Steiner, *Esoterische Unterweisungen für die erste Klasse der Freien Hochschule für Geisteswissenschaft am Goetheanum 1924*. CW 270b, pp. 60.

298   In regard to her specific spiritual situation at this period see the monograph, *Die letzten drei Jahre. Ita Wegman in Ascona 1940–1943*. Dornach 2006.

299   Ita Wegman, letter to Marianne Bischof, Dec.13, 1940. Ita Wegman Archive, Arlesheim.

300   Ita Wegman, letter to Madeleine van Deventer, Jan. 20, 1941. Ita Wegman Archive, Arlesheim.

301   Cf. Peter Selg, *Rudolf Steiner und die freie Hochschule für Geisteswissenschaft. Die Begründung der Ersten Klasse,* pp. 97f. As Marie Steiner recorded in one of her notebooks, Rudolf Steiner had already formulated guidelines for groups of people "who wish to engage in a living way with the mantric Class verses": "Those who spoke the mantras should elaborate what they had to say as a connecting link between them. He [Steiner] thus sought a kind of independent work on the verses, naturally without relinquishing the wisdom they preserved. But above all he wanted people to experience the mantras themselves" (Notebook 20, first published in the editor's foreword in Rudolf Steiner, *Esoterische Unterweisungen für die erste Klasse der Freien Hochschule für Geisteswissenschaft am Goetheanum 1924.* CW 270a, p. XIII). Cf. also Ita Wegman's letter to Willem Zeylmans van Emmichoven on 9.9.1925 in Peter Selg, *Rudolf Steiner und die Freie Hochschule für Geisteswissenschaft. Die Begründung der Ersten Klasse,* pp. 157f.

302   Cf. the discussion of these occurrences and the motives possibly guiding Rudolf Steiner in Peter Selg, *Rudolf Steiner und die Freie Hochschule für Geisteswissenschaft. Die Begründung der Ersten Klasse,* pp. 121ff. and pp. 153f.

303   In Peter Selg, *Die letzten drei Jahre. Ita Wegman in Ascona 1940–1943,* p. 94.

304   Rudolf Steiner, *Vorträge und Kurse über christlich-religiöses Wirken, V. Apokalypse und Priesterwirken.* CW 346. Dornach 2001, p. 87.

305   Rudolf Steiner, *Die Konstitution der Allgemeinen Anthroposophischen Gesellschaft und der Freien Hochschule für Geisteswissenschaft. Der Wiederaufbau des Goetheanum.* CW 260a, p. 77; author's emphasis.

306   Christian Morgenstern, *Werke und Briefe.* Vol. II. *Lyrik 1906–1914.* Stuttgart 1992, p. 251.

307   Rudolf Steiner, *Esoterische Unterweisungen für die erste Klasse der Freien Hochschule für Geisteswissenschaft am Goetheanum 1924.* CW 270a, p. 131.

308   Sergei O. Prokofieff, *Die Erste Klasse der Michael-Schule und ihre christologischen Grundlagen,* pp. 61f.

309 Ita Wegman Archive, Arlesheim. In J. Emanuel Zeylmans van Emmichoven, *Die Erkraftung des Herzens. Eine Mysterienschulung der Gegenwart. Rudolf Steiners Zusammenarbeit mit Ita Wegman*, pp. 407ff.

310 First published in Peter Selg, *Rudolf Steiner und Christian Rosenkreutz*. Arlesheim 2010, pp. 111–126.

311 Ita Wegman Archive, Arlesheim. In J. Emanuel Zeylmans van Emmichoven, *Die Erkraftung des Herzens. Eine Mysterienschulung der Gegenwart. Rudolf Steiners Zusammenarbeit mit Ita Wegman*, pp. 407ff.

312 Ita Wegman Archive, Arlesheim.

313 Ibid.

314 Documentation at the Goetheanum.

315 Minutes, p.256. Documentation at the Goetheanum.

316 Cf. J. Emanuel Zeylmans van Emmichoven, *Die Erkraftung des Herzens. Eine Mysterienschulung der Gegenwart. Rudolf Steiners Zusammenarbeit mit Ita Wegman*.

317 Ibid., pp. 177.

318 Emanuel Zeylmans van Emmichoven was unaware of Ita Wegman's statement on 11.29.1930 (according to which she possessed a written record of the cultic act that preceded the giving of the rose cross and the conferring of shared responsibility for the Class). It was only after Zeylmans's death when I was researching my study on Elisabeth Vreede (2009) that I discovered the quoted sentence in the meeting transcript at the Documentation archive at the Goetheanum. Emanuel Zeylmans never discussed whether the ritual preceding the giving of the rose cross was amongst Ita Wegman's esoteric papers. He published the text itself under the title of the "Great Rose Cross Meditation" in his compilation, but until the end was uncertain about its context and temporal locus ("Unfortunately it is not possible to date this great exercise. Seen in the context of the other exercises, I suspect that it originated in the fall of 1923." *Die Erkraftung des Herzens. Eine Mysterienschulung der Gegenwart. Rudolf Steiners Zusammenarbeit mit Ita Wegman*, p. 177).

319 See the handwritten texts by Rudolf Steiner and Ita Wegman, pp. [114]f.

320 See the numbering by Wegman and the comments on this by J. Emanuel Zeylmans van Emmichoven in, *Die Erkraftung des Herzens. Eine Mysterienschulung der Gegenwart. Rudolf Steiners Zusammenarbeit mit Ita Wegman*, p. 175.

321 In relation to the Christology of the cardiovascular system, cf. Peter Selg, *Vom Logos menschlicher Physis. Die Entfaltung einer anthroposophischen Humanphysiologie im Werk Rudolf Steiners,* vol. 2, pp. 817ff; and Peter Selg, *Mysterium cordis. Von der Mysterienstätte des Menschenherzens. Studien zu einer sakramentalen Physiologie des Herzorgans. Aristoteles—Thomas von Aquin—Rudolf Steiner.* Dornach 2006, pp. 125ff.

322 In J. Emanuel Zeylmans van Emmichoven, *Die Erkraftung des Herzens. Eine Mysterienschulung der Gegenwart. Rudolf Steiners Zusammenarbeit mit Ita Wegman,* p. 333.

323 Ibid., pp. 404ff.

324 Ita Wegman, letter to Albert Steffen, 3.16.1926. Ita Wegman Archive, Arlesheim. First published in J. Zeylmans van Emmichoven, *Wer war Ita Wegman. Eine Dokumentation.* Vol. 3, pp. 65ff. Thomas Meyer rightly pointed out that the ritual act was intended to lead to a deeper union of Ita Wegman with Christian Rosenkreutz, writing in this context: "That this inclusion of Wegman in the leadership of the Michael School literally occurred in the sign of the Rose Cross, also clarifies why in all repeated lessons in Dornach the Rosicrucian formula *'Ex deo nascimur / In Christo morimur / Per spiritum sanctum reviviscimus'* was added, as well as the corresponding three gestures. Michael impulse and Rosicrucianism thus became a unified overall impulse, and the mantric substance was given a still stronger protective mantle" (T. H. Meyer, "Die neue Rolle Ita Wegmans." In, *Der Meditationsweg der Michaelschule in neunzehn Stunden. Rudolf Steiners esoterisches Vermächtnis aus dem Jahre 1924.* Supplementary volume. Ed. Thomas Meyer, pp. 247f). For more on the spiritual aspects of the connection between the Michael School and the Rosicrucian stream within the First Class, see also the fundamental comments by Sergei O. Prokofieff, "Die Michael-Schule und die Rosenkreuzerströmung" in, *Die Erste Klasse der Michael-Schule und ihre christologischen Grundlagen,* pp. 369–441.

325 First published in *Das Goetheanum* no. 50, 2010, pp. 1–4.

326 Rudolf Steiner, *Die Weihnachtstagung zur Begründung der Allgemeinen Anthroposophischen Gesellschaft 1923/24.* CW 260, p. 46.

327 Rudolf Steiner, *Konferenzen mit den Lehrern der Freien Waldorfschule 1923–1924.* CW 300c. Dornach 1975, p. 114.

328 Ibid., p. 115.

329 Ibid., pp. 115f.

330 Ibid., p. 119.

331 Lilly Kolisko, *Eugen Kolisko. Ein Lebensbild.* Gerabronn-Crailsheim 1961, p. 90.

332 Rudolf Steiner to Lilly Kolisko. In Lilly Kolisko, letter to Ita Wegman, 11.2.1924. Ita Wegman Archive, Arlesheim.

333 For an account of the social efficacy of the Class lessons for the faculty, cf. Lilly Kolisko, letter to Ita Wegman 11.2.1924. Ita Wegman Archive, Arlesheim. Passages of this were published in Johannes Kiersch, *Zur Entwicklung der Freien Hochschule für Geisteswissenschaft. Die Erste Klasse.* Dornach 2005, pp. 94ff; and Peter Selg, *Rudolf Steiner und die Freie Hochschule für Geisteswissenschaft.* Arlesheim 2008, p. 120.

334 See Rudolf Steiner, *Die Methodik des Lehrens und die Lebensbedingungen des Erziehens.* CW 308. Dornach 1986, p. 93.

335 Unpublished. Ita Wegman Archive, Arlesheim.

336 For more on the situation among anthroposophic physicians at the beginning of 1924, see J. Emanuel Zeylmans van Emmichoven, *Wer war Ita Wegman. Eine Dokumentation.* Vol. I, pp. 128ff and Vol. 2, pp. 43ff. Also see Peter Selg (ed.), *Anthroposophische Ärzte. Lebens- und Arbeitswege im 20. Jahrhundert.* Dornach 2000.

337 Cf. Peter Selg, *Helene von Grunelius und Rudolf Steiners Kurse für die jungen Mediziner: Eine biographische Studie.* Dornach 2003.

338 Cf. Peter Selg, *"Die Medizin muss Ernst machen mit dem geistigen Leben." Rudolf Steiners Hochschulkurse für die "jungen Mediziner."* Dornach 2006.

339 Madeleine P. van Deventer, *Die anthroposophischemedizinische Bewegung in den verschiedenen Etappen ihrer Entwicklung.* Arlesheim 1982, p. 28.

340 Rudolf Steiner, *Esoterische Unterweisungen für die erste Klasse der Freien Hochschule für Geisteswissenschaft am Goetheanum 1924.* CW 270a, p. 149.

341 *Esoterische Unterweisungen für die erste Klasse der Freien Hochschule für Geisteswissenschaft am Goetheanum 1924.* CW 270c, p. 162.

342 Rudolf Steiner, *Meditative Betrachtungen und Anleitungen zur Vertiefung der Heilkunst. Vorträge für Ärzte und Medizinstudierende.* CW 316, p. 223.

343 Ibid., pp. 73f.

344 For more on the "esoteric core of the Medical Section," its development and aims, cf. Rudolf Steiner, *Das Zusammenwirken von Ärzten und Seelsorgern. Pastoral-Medizinischer Kurs.* CW 318. Dornach 1994, pp. 165f.; and Peter Selg, *Die Briefkorrespondenz der "jungen Mediziner". Eine dokumentarische Studie zur Rezeption*

von Rudolf Steiners "Jungmediziner"-Kursen. Dornach 2005, pp. 145ff.

345 Gottfried Husemann, "Die Begründung des Christengemeinschaft," in *Erinnerungen an Rudolf Steiner* (ed. Erika Beltle and Kurt Vierl. Stuttgart 1979, p. 311.)

346 Rudolf Steiner, *Konferenzen mir den Lehrern der Fereien Waldorf- schule 1923–1924.* CW 300c, p. 177.

347 Rudolf Steiner, *Vorträge und Kurse über christlich-religiöses Wirken, V. Apokalypse und Priesterwirken.* CW 346. Dornach 2001, p. 44.

348 Rudolf Steiner, *Mysterienstätten des Mittelalters. Rosenkreuzer- tum und modernes Einweihungsprinzip. Das Osterfest als ein Stück Mysteriengeschichte der Menschheit.* CW 233a. Dornach 1991, pp. 134f.

349 Rudolf Steiner, *Meditative Betrachtungen und Anleitungen zur Vertiefung der Heilkunst. Vorträge für Ärzte und Medizinstudier- ende,* CW 316, p. 220.

350 Rudolf Steiner, *Esoterische Unterweisungen für die erste Klasse der Freien Hochschule für Geisteswissenschaft am Goetheanum 1924.* CW 270a, p. 151.

Books in English Translation by Peter Selg

On Rudolf Steiner

Rudolf Steiner: Life and Work: *(1914–1918): The Years of World War I*, vol. 4 of 7 (2016)

Rudolf Steiner: Life and Work: *(1900–1914): Spiritual Science and Spiritual Community*, vol. 3 of 7 (2015)

Rudolf Steiner: Life and Work: *(1890–1900): Weimar and Berlin*, vol. 2 of 7 (2014)

Rudolf Steiner: Life and Work: *(1861–1890): Childhood, Youth, and Study Years*, vol. 1 of 7 (2014)

Rudolf Steiner and Christian Rosenkreutz (2012)

Rudolf Steiner as a Spiritual Teacher: *From Recollections of Those Who Knew Him* (2010)

On Christology

The Sufferings of the Nathan Soul: *Anthroposophic Christology on the Eve of World War I* (2016)

The Lord's Prayer and Rudolf Steiner: *A Study of His Insights into the Archetypal Prayer of Christianity* (2014)

The Creative Power of Anthroposophical Christology: *An Outline of Occult Science · The First Goetheanum · The Fifth Gospel · The Christmas Conference* (with Sergei O. Prokofieff) (2012)

Christ and the Disciples: *The Destiny of an Inner Community* (2012)

The Figure of Christ: Rudolf Steiner and the Spiritual Intention behind the Goetheanum's Central Work of Art (2009)

Rudolf Steiner and the Fifth Gospel: Insights into a New Understanding of the Christ Mystery (2010)

Seeing Christ in Sickness and Healing (2005)

ON GENERAL ANTHROPOSOPHY

The Destiny of the Michael Community: Foundation Stone for the Future (2014)

Spiritual Resistance: Ita Wegman 1933–1935 (2014)

The Last Three Years: Ita Wegman in Ascona, 1940–1943 (2014)

From Gurs to Auschwitz: The Inner Journey of Maria Krehbiel-Darmstädter (2013)

Crisis in the Anthroposophical Society: And Pathways to the Future (2013); with Sergei O. Prokofieff

Rudolf Steiner's Foundation Stone Meditation: And the Destruction of the Twentieth Century (2013)

The Culture of Selflessness: Rudolf Steiner, the Fifth Gospel, and the Time of Extremes (2012)

The Mystery of the Heart: The Sacramental Physiology of the Heart in Aristotle, Thomas Aquinas, and Rudolf Steiner (2012)

Rudolf Steiner and the School for Spiritual Science: The Foundation of the "First Class" (2012)

Rudolf Steiner's Intentions for the Anthroposophical Society: The Executive Council, the School for Spiritual Science, and the Sections (2011)

The Fundamental Social Law: Rudolf Steiner on the Work of the Individual and the Spirit of Community (2011)

The Path of the Soul after Death: *The Community of the Living and the Dead as Witnessed by Rudolf Steiner in his Eulogies and Farewell Addresses* (2011)

The Agriculture Course, Koberwitz, Whitsun 1924: *Rudolf Steiner and the Beginnings of Biodynamics* (2010)

On Anthroposophical Medicine and Curative Education

Honoring Life: *Medical Ethics and Physician-Assisted Suicide* (2014); with Sergei O. Prokofieff

I Am for Going Ahead: *Ita Wegman's Work for the Social Ideals of Anthroposophy* (2012)

The Child with Special Needs: *Letters and Essays on Curative Education* (Ed.) (2009)

Ita Wegman and Karl König: *Letters and Documents* (2008)

Karl König's Path to Anthroposophy (2008)

Karl König: My Task: *Autobiography and Biographies* (Ed.) (2008)

On Child Development and Waldorf Education

I Am Different from You: *How Children Experience Themselves and the World in the Middle of Childhood* (2011)

Unbornness: *Human Pre-existence and the Journey toward Birth* (2010)

The Essence of Waldorf Education (2010)

The Therapeutic Eye: *How Rudolf Steiner Observed Children* (2008)

A Grand Metamorphosis: *Contributions to the Spiritual-Scientific Anthropology and Education of Adolescents* (2008)

Ita Wegman Institute
for Basic Research into Anthroposophy

Pfeffinger Weg 1a, ch 4144 Arlesheim, Switzerland
www.wegmaninstitut.ch
e-mail: sekretariat@wegmaninstitut.ch

The Ita Wegman Institute for Basic Research into Anthroposophy is a non-profit research and teaching organization. It undertakes basic research into the lifework of Dr. Rudolf Steiner (1861–1925) and the application of Anthroposophy in specific areas of life, especially medicine, education, and curative education. Work carried out by the Institute is supported by a number of foundations and organizations and an international group of friends and supporters. The Director of the Institute is Prof. Dr. Peter Selg.

www.ingramcontent.com/pod-product-compliance
Lightning Source LLC
Chambersburg PA
CBHW020157090426
42734CB00008B/855